Representing
Men

Representing
Men

Maleness and
Masculinity in
the **Media**

Kenneth MacKinnon

ARNOLD

First published in Great Britain in 2003 by
Arnold, a member of the Hodder Headline Group,
338 Euston Road, London NW1 3BH

http://www.arnoldpublishers.com

Distributed in the United States of America by
Oxford University Press Inc.,
198 Madison Avenue, New York, NY10016

British Library Cataloguing in Publication Data
A catalogue record for this book is available from the British Library

Library of Congress Cataloging-in-Publication Data
A catalog record for this book is available from the Library of Congress

ISBN 0 340 80832 2 (hb)
ISBN 0 340 80833 0 (pb)

1 2 3 4 5 6 7 8 9 10

Typeset in 9.5/12.5 New Baskerville by Charon Tec Pvt. Ltd, Chennai, India
Printed and bound in Great Britain by MPG Books Ltd, Bodmin, Cornwall.

What do you think about this book? Or any other Arnold title?
Please send your comments to feedback.arnold@hodder.co.uk

CONTENTS

ACKNOWLEDGEMENTS

It would have been difficult, if not impossible, to write this book without the considerable help of Learning Centre staff from the former University of North London (now London Metropolitan University), particularly in terms of inter-library loans. A similar debt of gratitude is owed to the former Faculty of Humanities and Teacher Education's Research Committee for its valuable granting of research-relief resourcing to me.

The author and publishers would like to thank the following individuals and institutions for permission to reproduce copyright illustrative material:

The Advertising Archives Ltd. for figure 6.1, bfi Collections for figures 4.2, 4.3, 5.1, 5.2, and 5.3, Phil Walter/Empics for figure 7.1, The Kobal Collection/20th Century Fox Television/Feingold, Deborah for figure 5.4, National Film Archive for figure 4.1 and Richard Young/Rex Features for figure 7.2.

INTRODUCTION

When the word 'gender' or the term 'gender studies' is used, readers tend to think that a discussion of women will follow. Yet, men are gendered. Masculinity is unlikely to be an aspect of biology or nature, but popular thought sometimes believes that it is beyond question or analysis, that it is not so much dominant as 'normal'.

There are additional reasons why men and their masculinity have evaded the sorts of questioning applied to women and their femininity or to homosexuality. Feminism, which has led the way in exploration of gender, historically applied most of its initial energy to conceptions and depictions of women and femininity. Gay studies was more concerned with considering societal reactions to homosexuality than to heterosexuality. This meant that, for a time at least, masculinity and one of its traditional components, male heterosexuality, escaped notice, and could continue to pose as the natural norm.

This book attempts to explore the long-protected mysteries of masculinity and, in particular, to chart its representation in popular culture, especially from the 1980s onwards. It falls into two halves. Part A deals with general questions surrounding men and masculinity, and those concerning representation and spectatorship. Part B looks at four different aspects of the mass media in order to consider the representation of masculinity in each: film, television, advertising and mediated sport.

The opening chapter of Part A attempts to understand the nature of masculinity. It begins by considering whether gender is a matter of nature or of social education. It then goes on to suggest the plurality of masculinities and to explore the notion and point of 'hegemonic' masculinity, incorporating ideals and myths towards which 'actual' masculinities may strive but not achieve. The components of masculinity are viewed with particular emphasis on questions of its relation to violence and to femininity.

Chapter 2 highlights the growth, within the past decade, of men's studies programmes in universities and of so-called men's movements within wider society. The two phenomena could be distinguished, broadly, by the attention given by the former to the realization that men are socially gendered; the latter, particularly in the case of movements inspired by Robert Bly's *Iron John*, tends contrastingly to think of masculinity as a sort of eternal essence which has been recently denied to men by the over-influence of feminist thinking.

Part A ends with Chapter 3's investigation of representation and spectatorship. In relation to the former, it considers the drawback with content analyses, that a norm of masculinity is assumed against which media depictions are categorized as, for example, positive or negative. Film studies – especially Laura Mulvey's work – on cinema spectatorship suggests that looking is not a straightforward matter, but that it vitally concerns and relates to gender. Mulvey's conclusions are themselves suggested to be too schematic in, for instance, rejecting the possibility of a male, as well as a female, object of the gaze.

Part B considers actual representation of men and their masculinity in four different contexts. Chapter 4 focuses on films, and offers analyses of genres, stars and individual movies in relation to the shifting versions of masculinity on offer between the 1970s and 1980s into the 1990s and the new millennium.

Television is considered next, in Chapter 5. The peculiar nature of commercial television's 'flow' is analysed, so that various kinds of masculinity may be studied in different temporal contexts. Some of the most valuable work seems to have centred on 1980s' series, the decade of Reaganism providing a sharp contrast with the preceding world under Carter or the less 'yuppified' US of the 1990s.

Advertising, if only because it deals with 'gendered' products traditionally thought to appeal to either male or female consumers – but only recently to both at once – must construct versions of the masculine with particular appeal to male or female consumers, or both. Chapter 6 investigates the sorts of masculinity constructed for the delectation of women or, in the case of beer and car commercials, to reinforce notions of hegemonic masculinity.

Mediated sports (that is sport as presented on television or described in newspapers' sports sections, say) are discussed in relation to masculinity in the seventh and final chapter of the book. So strong is the link between these sports and masculinity that gender seems to be 'invisible' unless women are playing, and sport is taken to be educative, providing a form of initiation for boys into the world of men.

The Wider Questions:
Men/Masculinity/Representation

Chapter One

Masculinity

SEX AND GENDER: MALENESS AND MASCULINITY

All known societies distinguish between male and female. All known societies also provide their males and females with models of behaviour deemed appropriate to these sexes – in other words, with notions of masculinity and femininity that a culture largely consents to and upholds.

These gender ideals vary with the passage of time. For instance, during World War II American and British women might have been expected to take on factory work and to view their domestic duties as secondary; yet, by the 1950s there were strenuous efforts by the popular media to create guilt in women who chose careers over home-making and motherhood.

The ideals also vary from culture to culture, though social science would agree that there are significant similarities across cultures regarding the standard conceptions of masculinity and femininity. This does not, however, answer the question of whether gender is 'natural' – an 'essence' (so that males are, as it were, programmed at birth to be masculine) – or 'learned' (acquired by a process of social education, initially via the family).

There can be no doubt of the scale and tenacity of the belief that men cannot fundamentally change, that there is a fixed masculinity. A wide spectrum of modern society embraces this view, including Christian fundamentalists, feminist essentialists, and the *Iron John*-inspired men's movement (discussed in Chapter 2). This belief seeks to justify itself in terms of such things as hormones and anatomy. There is indeed some biological justification for, say, linking testosterone, the chief male sex hormone, with masculine aggression. How far, though, can biology explain the great variety of male social behaviour or render male social privilege beyond question on the grounds that it is founded in human nature?

Those thinkers – evolutionary biologists, for example – who do believe that sexual behaviour has its foundation in biology make direct comparisons between animals and human beings to arrive at an understanding of it. Disturbing phenomena such as rape are explained in terms of a male 'sex drive' which is presumably, because believed natural, ultimately unstoppable. How, though, does a biological explanation make sense of those societies with markedly lower rape statistics than others? If masculinity appears as something of a social problem, as it does in the instances of rape or football hooliganism, believers in male nature turn for their answers to biochemistry or genetics. By denying or downplaying the learning of masculinity through socialization, they effectively undermine the lessons that could be learned from the study of psychology or sociology.

There are at least two extreme tendencies in those who enter the nature/nurture debate regarding gender. One school of thought favours a notion of sex polarity – in other words, the sexes are radically divided and continue to be so throughout adult life. The other school of thought believes in sex neutrality, and would have it that undifferentiated human material has sex differences, real or presumed, imposed on it from birth onwards.

The nature/nurture debate might surely be more usefully conducted with attention to both elements. While biology is likely to determine certain aspects of gender, surely a significant proportion of gender belief and behaviour is best explained with reference to the social. Arthur Brittan makes the case eloquently:

> Biology and society are never separate – they mutually constitute each other. Hence, the 'true facts' of biology are never pristine and uninterpreted. They are always mediated. The 'facts' of sexual difference are 'facts' by virtue of ... generalized belief ...

(Brittan, 1989, p. 14)

The 'gender system', which seems so significant for so many societies, forbids the sameness of male and female. There are social rewards for being 'real' men or 'real' women. It is not surprising, therefore, that in society actual men and women present themselves, and demand to be perceived, as 'real'. This helps to make sense of the wide insistence on the naturalness of sexual difference as a fact. Yet, the insistence is on a belief, rather than a fact.

For many academic writers, gender is a matter of power relations, a system that categorizes people as distinct groups, male and female. They believe that gender, being a power relation, has to be negotiated and renegotiated, rather than accepted passively as if it were a human trait.

Karl Marx believed that it is not just groups subordinated in a system of domination that are damaged, but that the dominant group is also damaged. The notion of 'alienation' was used by him in the sense of a process through which one becomes a stranger to oneself, and one's powers become powers ranged over and against oneself.

Marx was attempting to provide this concept of alienation with a particular context, that of capitalism, and to relate it to both workers and capitalists. Harry Brod, however, makes use of the concept in a new context, that of patriarchy. His argument is that men, and male sexuality especially, come to be alienated, in a Marxist sense, in the system of patriarchy, even though it is normally taken to benefit males and subordinate females (Brod, in Hearn and Morgan (eds), 1990, pp. 126–127). Despite his concern for the way that male sexuality involves alienation under the gender system, a great deal of literature on sexuality takes no account of such aspects of the construction of gendered identity. (Conversely, a great deal of literature on gender takes no account of sexuality.)

A key thinker in the matter of the construction of gender and sexuality is the French philosopher Michel Foucault. Foucault selects *discourse* as the way in which this construction may best be understood. By this, he appears to mean that social practices are constructed by the way that they can be spoken or thought about – conceptualized – in language. Discourse ultimately enforces 'normalcy'. For Foucault, gender and sexuality are discourses that are entwined and mutually sustaining.

Foucault's 'subject', the human individual, has many identities. One important method by which the subject acquires an identity is by differentiating itself from what is believed in discourse to be its opposite. So, because 'masculine' and 'feminine' are talked about as being opposed to each other in much the way that 'male' and 'female' are, the acquisition of male identity involves insisting on distance from the female subject and her femininity. It also involves devaluation of the believed binary opposites, femaleness and femininity. The instability of our 'selves', to follow Foucault's reasoning, demands an investment in our distinctness, together with a disparaging of that from which we would like to be seen as distinct.

In the 1990s, so-called 'queer theory' built on such foundations as those provided by Foucault to offer a new explanation of identity, and in particular of gendered identity. It is not that we *are* our identity; rather, we *perform* our identity. Thus, we perform our gender and our sexuality. By these performances, we keep the system(s) of gender and sexuality alive. Queer theory ultimately suggests that gender can be changed. The 'laws' of gender are formed simply by continual performances of gender. At the very least, the awareness of gender as 'performative' suggests its instability – why else would it require constant reworking?

The male body takes on a crucial role in masculinity. Because the body is so obviously there, and it is so obviously physical, the suggestion is that if it is male, its masculinity is natural. Yet, the body is also, in Michael Messner's words, 'an object of social practice' (1990, p. 214). This could be illustrated with reference to the role that, for example, weight-training, exercise and steroids play in the social construction of the body.

Murray Healey uses the example of Marky Mark (aka Mark Wahlberg) to show that 'hypermasculinity' (the exaggerated display of what are culturally taken to be macho traits) overcompensates. His macho dress codes, his gym-created body, his near-nakedness, are parts of the means by which the star declares his machismo. However, hypermasculinity exposes, rather than allays, anxiety about masculinity. There is clearly, for Healey, a contradiction in *trying* to be a real man, since this exposes the real man's reality as an achievement, not a biological fact. Of Marky Mark, he writes, 'The more he resorts to his body as proof of his virility, the more he "unmans" himself, in effect admitting that his only asset is his body – the traditional position of female stars' (Healey, 1994, p. 88).

MASCULINITY: A PSYCHOANALYTIC ACCOUNT

The concepts of masculinity and femininity were causes of perhaps surprising perplexity to Sigmund Freud, the founder of psychoanalysis. He recognized that these concepts were multiple and that, for instance, psychology, biology and sociology understood them in distinct ways. He did not, though, resolve the problem of how to tie up these varying notions of gender into a coherent whole. One particular understanding of masculine and feminine for Freud was as metaphors for 'active' and 'passive' respectively.

Crucially, he did not accept that either masculinity or femininity existed in a pure state. No individual was, for Freud, purely masculine or purely feminine. It surely follows, therefore, that maleness and masculinity must have been distinguishable for him. Freud believed that femininity had to be part of a man's character – as, therefore, had passivity.

One explanation for this inevitable component of femininity in a man's psychological make-up was the male infant's identification with his mother in early life. During this period, the infant was unable, Freud argued, to distinguish himself from his mother.

Jacques Lacan christened this state of feeling at one with the mother the 'imaginary order'. The 'symbolic order' for him is one in which, for example, the separateness of 'I', 'you', 'he/she/it' is recognized. Until that recognition, language is impossible. Both male and female infants need to progress psychologically to that order to become socialized and to be able to use language. For the male, though, this progression involves the pain of giving up unity with the mother. The child learns to walk and talk, to perform independent actions, but in so doing he has to suffer the pangs of separation from her. To be an individual, he obviously has to be individuated.

In Freudian and post-Freudian understanding, apart from Lacan's, the male's progress to selfhood is always at the cost of unity with the mother. In other words, to achieve masculinity, in its senses of independence, activity and self-assuredness, he has to distance himself from the femininity represented in its strongest form by his mother. In this sense, psychoanalysis suggests that masculinity necessarily involves a distancing from and distrust of femininity.

Some post-Freudians would have it that a powerful adult male fantasy involves a return to the symbiotic relationship with his mother that the male child once enjoyed. Whatever its appeal, though, the fantasy must be accompanied with fear – the fear that a restoration of unity with the mother will bring about the destruction of selfhood. In other words, as anthropologist David Gilmore puts it, manhood imagery is, from a post-Freudian perspective, a defence against the eternal child within the man (Gilmore, 1990, p. 29). ('Manhood imagery' may loosely be understood as that which is designed to boost machismo. Its basis is in an overvaluing of the penis, so that it is no longer a vulnerable male organ but converted into the phallus of masculine myth.)

Psychonalysis appears to teach us that even the outwardly most masculine of men have a hidden, guarded, soft emotional element within their psychology. This 'femininity' is vigorously repressed because, for reasons offered above, it is perceived as a threat to the very masculinity by which men seek to measure their achievement. Nevertheless, masculinity is an ideal, not an actuality. Men's experience must always fall short. Masculinity is just out of reach. It becomes *ideological*, a goal to strive towards, but not ultimately attainable. Thus, being a 'real man' is precarious, always under threat, even from within. It involves struggle.

The male rejection of the mother and repression of the feminine within himself can result in women being taken as embodiments of that which is rejected and repressed. What a man fears within himself – vulnerability, sentiment, emotion, commitment – is often projected outwards on to women and homosexual men and vehemently denied.

Psychoanalytic accounts of masculinity suggest explanations in psychic development for its defensive, repressed aspect. Yet, both maleness and masculinity are often treated as a norm, as if these were a matter of genetic programming.

MASCULINITY DEFINED IN TERMS OF ITS EXCLUSIONS

As the psychoanalytic account above suggests, masculinity acquires a shape and becomes definable in terms of what it denies that it is. Masculinity may be understood partly by contrast with what is excluded from it – the feminine.

Femininity is taken to apply to the world of women, most obviously. It is taken also to apply to homosexual males, to whom culture often imputes effeminacy. Publicly defining oneself as heterosexual seems to be a means to male legitimacy. The ostentatious display in the workplace of pin-ups of women can serve to advertise this badge of legitimacy, feeding back into the social with widespread objectification of women and stigmatization of men whose heterosexuality is deemed not to be above suspicion.

The fear of homosexuality that seems intrinsic to normative masculinity has another explanation – that passive anal intercourse is seen as disturbingly feminizing. The reason is obvious. Heterosexual intercourse has been explained in ideological terms by, for example, Catherine Walby as asserting not just women's penetrability but men's impenetrability (Catherine Walby, in Grosz and Probyn (eds), 1995, p. 272).

The ideology of sexual intercourse and its relation with heterosexuality, and thus with masculinity, may help to explain men's difficulty in coming to terms with the need for

7

prostate-cancer checks, for instance. Despite the prevalence of the disease, resistance to checks seems to focus on the sense of outrage that digital examination of the patient's lower bowel produces in many men. (Reluctance to undergo investigation must also, of course, be linked with fear of impotence as a result of surgery for prostate cancer.)

Broadly, fear of the feminine, both within men and also external to them in society, combines dread of passivity and a denial of narcissism (pleasure in one's appearance) and of exhibitionism (pleasure in being looked at). This last is peculiarly disorienting in the 1990s, when it is claimed that there was a fashion crossover between gay and straight styles. 'Poofs can look like real men,' Murray Healey asserts, '... therefore, real men look like poofs' (1994, p. 94). As early as the 1970s, the process of disorientation began with what might be called the 'machoization' of male homosexual culture. What was a bid to shake off the stigma of effeminacy had, as an effect, immersion into what could be interpreted as the downside of masculinity: a widespread aversion to intimacy or emotional commitment.

Male friendship is dogged by fear of being thought homosexual, it would seem. The verbal intimacy customary between female friends is markedly less frequent among self-identifying heterosexual male friends. Talk there concerns primarily work and sport, as well as complaints about and worries over women. This is not to say that there may not be profound bonding between men. Rather, interaction is guarded and talk avoids the intimate.

As a paradoxical footnote to this account, it would seem to be, despite all the attempts to assert that masculinity has nothing to do with women and homosexual men, the combined forces of feminism and gay culture that have made masculinity visible, and thus most open to discussion and analysis.

Nevertheless, until the 1990s masculinity was largely treated within feminism as if it were unconstructed. Feminism habitually, but particularly in the 1970s, deconstructed images of women and distrusted explanations for these based on 'the natural'. Its comparative lack of interest in deconstructing images of men may have been for the good reason of not wishing to divert attention from the feminist work that still needed to be done on women. It had, though, the effect of allowing masculinity to continue to be seen as a natural, rather than cultural, phenomenon. Simone de Beauvoir observes, 'A man would never get the notion of writing a book on the peculiar situation of the human male' (Simone de Beauvoir, in Gerzon, 1982, p. 1). Only rarely, though, before the 1990s would a woman get this notion either.

One effect of inattention to masculinity as a construct is that the privilege of white men at least is allowed to remain invisible and thus beyond discussion. Or, more colourfully, the discussion of it is written off, as it has been allegedly by Australian men when they call it women's or poofter talk (Lewis, 1983, p. 10). It is a short step to taking male privilege, if it cannot be looked at squarely in terms of its construction, as a matter of nature – and thus beyond useful discussion.

HEGEMONIC MASCULINITY

'Hegemony' is a term that was originally used by Antonio Gramsci in the course of analysing Italian class relations. It became possibly his most important contribution to Marxist thinking. By means of hegemony arguments, he moved away from class-against-class analysis in favour of attention to 'the popular'. R. W. Connell explains its usage to signify 'a social ascendancy achieved in a play of social forces that extends beyond contests of brute power into the organization of private life and cultural processes' (1987, p. 184). Thus, for him, the term does not apply easily to ascendancy achieved by arms or by the threat of unemployment, for example. Rather, the ascendancy deserving of this description is 'embedded', to use Connell's expression, in religious doctrine and practice and mass media content, for instance. It involves persuasion – particularly by means of media – of the bulk of the population that certain social institutions are 'normal' or 'natural'. In other words, certain assumptions become popularized as common sense.

The appeal of the concept of hegemony to analysts of masculinity should be obvious. 'Hegemonic masculinity' was so named first by Connell in 1987, and was thus introduced to sociologists of gender. It was applied to the set of assumptions and beliefs about masculinity that pass as common sense.

An important distinction was made from the start between hegemonic masculinity and notions of 'male role'. The latter relates to social ideals to which male behaviour is expected to aspire, if not actually encompass. The former was and continues to be seen as a name for a particular variety of masculinity to which women and, among others, homosexual or effeminate men were subordinated. It provides a definition of what it means to be a man, and not coincidentally appears to ensure the dominance of some men within the sex/gender system. Study of hegemonic masculinity aims normally at identification of those sorts of men who enjoy power and wealth. It also attempts to delineate how social relationships which allow them dominance are made to seem legitimate and thus unquestioned.

Crucially, then, the culturally idealized form of masculinity may not be the usual form of masculinity actually practised within a society's history at a particular time. The actual personalities of the majority of men may show little correspondence with the cultural ideals of masculinity. It may be, in fact, that hegemony needs fantasy figures to embody its particular variety of masculinity. It could even be argued that too close an identification of men with hegemonic masculinity constitutes a health risk, since it is not difficult to sustain an argument that men are more physically vulnerable than women (men generally die younger and are more susceptible to heart attacks than women).

Hegemonies of various sorts are given shape in popular culture by journalists, politicians, mass media. Masculine hegemony is formed from the people's common sense by, perhaps above all, television, film, advertising and sport as relayed to and received

9

by huge audiences. (These highly important areas will be treated in separate chapters later in the book.) Media can, though, also help to create and bolster the audience's common sense.

Hegemonic masculinity is a slippery notion, rendered more complicated by the already noted possibility of difference between actual, socially practised masculinity and the idealized variety. Particularly excluded from hegemonic masculinity, or by means of it, are black and working-class men, as well as homosexual men. Though not all men practise it, it would be fair, nonetheless, to observe that most men benefit from hegemonic masculinity. Though it subordinates women, it should be conceded that so too may non-hegemonic masculinities.

What renders it even more slippery is that, as many commentators note, the survival of hegemonic masculinity depends on a form of incorporation of critiques of it. According to Christopher Newfield, 'Only feminization enables men ... to occupy both sides of a question. Whereas tyranny depends on male supremacy, liberal hegemony or "consensus" depends on male femininity' (Christopher Newfield, in Gallagher, 1992, p. 7). According to this thinking, masculinity is enabled to go on being hegemonic by incorporating the feminine. This, incidentally, helps to make fuller sense of David Gilmore's conclusion that one aspect of manhood is that it is a nurturing concept. He explains his notion of the nurturing element in man as follows:

> Men nurture their society by shedding their blood, their sweat, and their semen, by bringing home food for both child and mother, by producing children, and by dying if necessary in faraway places to provide a safe haven for their people. This, too, is nurturing in the sense of endowing or increasing.
>
> (Gilmore, 1990, p. 230)

Through such interpretations of idealized masculinity as incorporating the traditionally feminine trait of nurturing, it might be argued that masculinity holds on to its hegemony. This makes sense of the creation of the 'New Man' (to be discussed later in this chapter) at a time when the traditions of idealized masculinity were being severely critiqued by, above all, feminist writers.

This last example suggests that hegemonic masculinity is not to be approached as an unchanging entity, above and beyond history, and thus ahistorical. Recent writers would argue that this form of hegemony has constantly to be renegotiated within an ever-changing social structure. After all, it is best understood in relation to what it excludes and what it seeks to dominate. Put simply, if hegemonic masculinity is a means for certain men to dominate women and other men, then as these latter categories change so must the former category. Feminism, gay studies and queer theory respond to, but also create, the possibility of altered experiences and perceptions among the subordinated. Historical change among the subordinated seems to demand change in the dominant if that dominance is not to be radically destabilized.

MASCULINITIES, NOT MASCULINITY

By this last argument, hegemonic masculinity necessarily alters over time and amid changing circumstances. It cannot, by that understanding, be a monolith, but is protean – changing shape and emphasis – and also plural. Postmodernism, whose main focus is on instability and multiplicity, increases the already clearly discernible tendency to question the social norm of masculinity.

Subordinated masculinities have always been understood as plural. They would include, for example – to name but a few of those that spring to mind in the twenty-first century – gay, black and working-class masculinities. A great variety of masculinities has been created by such social factors as class, ethnicity, sexual orientation, able-bodiedness, religion, age.

To return for a moment to Foucauldian thinking, masculinity is, like gender in general and sexuality too, discourse. The very fact that discourses are subject to change means that masculinity, subordinated and dominant/idealized/hegemonic varieties alike, changes – and is of necessity plural.

MASCULINITY'S RELATION WITH VIOLENCE

A persistent cultural belief is that there is an almost unbreakable relationship between men and violence. As Glen Lewis says, 'Within certain limits, aggressive male behaviour is accepted as a normal part of everyday life' (1983, p. 11).

The reason for part of the huge public appeal of such areas as sport could be that it gives masculine aggression the chance of a legitimized, ritualized outlet. Violent aggression in sport is positively rewarded by commendation from other players on the same side, by coaches and sports fans. Because it is 'contained' by the rules of the game, such violence is offered a certain morality. Moreover, it is normally violence between men exclusively.

It has been argued that sport in this way helps to shore up masculine identity, by supplying visible proof, as it were, of men's natural physical superiority. The masculinity of the world of sport is particularly evident when it provides an exclusively male space for players, and what turns out to be a predominantly male space for sports fans. Moreover, in spite of the achievements of sportswomen, the rules of games are largely a male creation, designed to reward masculine skills. Also, watchers of televised sports are demonstrably far more interested in, and respectful of, male than female sports.

Perhaps aggressiveness in sport and lethal aggression from movie superheroes – Arnold Schwarzenegger as the original Terminator, for example – could be seen as the more acceptable face of male violence. The less acceptable face could be identified as violent crime. According to the FBI in 1992, about 90 per cent of violent crime was committed by males.

R. W. Connell goes so far as to suggest a link between, on the one hand, waning confidence in masculine power in social terms and, on the other, the growth in popularity of images of masculine potency in the media: 'With the gradually increasing pressure for gender equality, it seems, a market was created for representations of power in the arena men could still claim as distinctively their own, plain violence' (Connell, 1989, p. 215).

Violence appears largely to be gender-specific, both within society and in media representations of it or in its heroization in sport. Yet, debates about it tend to be gender neutral. One effect of this is the discussion of violence as if it were a social problem, rather than as if masculinity were the problem.

An important explanation for the prevalence and lovingly detailed and highlighted representation of violence in movies again implicates masculinity. This is that, without 'megaviolence', the bodies of such stars as Schwarzenegger, Sylvester Stallone and Jean-Claude Van Damme might be too obviously exposed as objects of fascinated audience interest. To ward off the threat of homoeroticism from such bodies, which are sometimes stripped fully naked in the course of their narratives, movies have to find an alibi for their concentrated attention to spectacular star bodies. That the alibi is often graphic violence surely suggests a close link between it and the imagined assertion through violence of unblemished masculinity for these heroes.

This is not, of course, to say that the lives of most men involve physical violence. Socially privileged, upper-middle-class men may experience and embody aggression in the boardroom and in career terms, but competition is not normally settled by physical fights. Nevertheless, representations of physical violence could have ideological and psychological significance for them. Surely, Rambo could not have achieved his enormous popularity in the 1980s without the emotional involvement of more than what are imagined to be 'working-class tough guys'.

It seems to be culturally believed that violence is a natural, practically genetic component of masculinity. The strength of that belief does not silence the viability of the persistent counter-view, that violence is learned, and that some men learn better than others, or that learning has a relation with systems of rewards and punishments. (We have already noted that effective sporting aggression is widely admired and positively valued within the world of professional sport itself.)

If, too, the more acceptable face of masculine violence involves physical struggle among strong adult males only, the belief in natural male violence has more unsettling implications. Violence in society involves wife-beating, rape, child abuse. It may be hard to credit that gender beliefs could play a significant part in condoning male violence of this variety. Nevertheless, they clearly do. Why else the importance of 'provocation' as a judicial defence in rape trials? Why else the effectiveness of the 'homosexual advance' plea as mitigation for murder?

The psychological importance of a sense of real or fantasized physical power becomes more acute when masculinity feels eroded or, to use a term often resorted to in academic writing on gender, 'in crisis'. Feminist analyses of patriarchy delineate the world as one in which power remains stubbornly with one gender and kept away from another. These analyses are persuasive, until at least the 1980s, when mass unemployment drove a wedge between masculine power and one of its rationalizations, the male as breadwinner. The wide feminist assumption – that men, because patriarchy ensures that they retain power, therefore *feel* powerful – is less persuasive. It is possible to argue that the glamorization of male violence is less a proof of men's arrogant basking in their power than a sign of their perception of growing social weakness and instability. At one time in history, men who experienced economic disaster could head for the 'frontier' on the North American sub-continent or the outposts of the British Empire, say, to take on what were conceived as the forces of Nature. Where are these frontiers today? They have to be reinvented in the guises of outer space or the so-called Third World.

The socio-economic changes of the 1980s and 1990s have been so radical as to produce men who, Rosalind Coward believes, are now in the same critical position as women were twenty years previously (1999, p. 59). One of the most cogent indications of the alterations in male self-perception comes from advertising. In the field of commercials, it has become a cliché today that men are domestically incompetent, insensitive, superficial and downright stupid. These depictions would clearly be abandoned if the result of them were loss of revenue for the products advertised. The tenacity of this advertising suggests that men collude in their vilification. The attempted revival of 'laddishness' in such British television sitcoms as *Men Behaving Badly*, or in the immensely popular American *The Simpsons* (with Bart as unregenerately laddish while Homer is stupid) suggests male awareness that they cannot unreflectively *be* laddish in actuality. A distance has been created from what might have once been taken as typical male conduct and character. One journalist believes that the male who is most loved today in the United Kingdom, to judge by the evidence of movies and television, is the 'bewildered bloke' with a sad little boy by his side (Landesman, 2002).

THE NEW MAN AND OTHER 'SOFT MASCULINITIES'

The so-called 'new man' was created first in the 1970s but has been recreated in a variety of forms since then. He would seem to be a middle-class professional, white, heterosexual, aged usually between mid-twenties and early forties, with a female partner – not necessarily wife – who has imbibed feminist ideas. Such information about him can be gleaned from 'lifestyle' men's magazines in particular. Traditional masculinity has been revised by the 'new man', so that he embodies the sort of anti-sexism which is characterized by his attempts to form non-oppressive relationships with women, children and other men. The evidence from the magazines is that there is an attempt to blur the traditional distinction between leisure and work. Yet, the clarity of his success at work, indicated by his relative affluence and interest in consumer goods, suggests that struggle and domination must be part of the new man's life experience, if not exactly lifestyle. There must be some sort of challenge to his emotional sensitivity implied, if not acknowledged, from his competitiveness in the workplace.

The new man, in his relations with women, tends to disavow the traditional link between sexual desire and female objectification. Yet, the tone of not just men's magazines, but the glossies aimed at 'new' women, usually shows suspicion of feminism, which sensitized everybody to female objectification from the 1970s onwards.

One of the ways in which sexuality is rethought in this context is in its links with fatherhood and reproduction. But perhaps it is the 'new father' image, not the underlying realities of such fatherhood, that is potent. There does not seem to have been a radical reconsideration of parenting in line with the new imagery. The advertising for the magazines showcases father/baby photographs. There are signs in the growth of a father's rights movement, which seeks to change the law to reduce women's control over children and childcare, that these images are not entirely divorced from social action. Yet, the material benefits and privilege on which the new man's lifestyle is so dependent do not seem to be questioned. Would not shared parenting as a social fact be bound to alter the masculinity that seems to be promoted in advertisements less concerned with parenting?

It might be easier to justify an idea of the new man as representing less a real shift in gender relations, than an updating of the 'old man' without the sexism – or rather, with a new sexual explicitness which, for example, objectifies men as well as women. The cruciality of advertising revenue for such magazines must mean that the masculinity on offer with the new man is rooted in consumerism. All the same, his creation must also surely indicate public acknowledgment of yet another crisis of masculinity. Men once lived in what could be thought of as ungendered space. That is, masculinity was deemed so natural, biologically given and predictable, that it did not undergo the examination that femininity was given, especially by feminism. Now, though, men show signs of being aware of having and performing (or not performing) roles. Masculinity has become, for men now as it has been for women, an enigma, a puzzling condition.

As consideration of the new man suggests above, perhaps it is the packaging of male power that changes rather than power itself. Masculinity may be expressed (packaged) in different ways at different times. 'Soft' masculinities are versions that are less oppressive. However, General Schwarzkopf's tears, shed publicly on television, suggest to Maurizia Boscagli that feminized emotions are used by such powerful men in a bid to produce what she calls 'a discourse of universality' – but which applies only to men! Schwarzkopf's transgression of the masculine gender role by public weeping is given a 'universal' interpretation. The General is taken as representative of 'humanity', although she believes that the universal human subject is a fiction. The Army remains extremely homophobic, she comments. Only those men and women who respect the gender distinctions that the General's tears seemed to destabilize are welcomed into it (Boscagli, 1992–93, p. 74).

Whatever the credibility of this analysis of a particular television moment, many other commentators voice suspicion of the way that masculinity may soften, become more feminine, without addressing patriarchal power or capitalist work relations. This softening of masculinity may have little to do with female emancipation or empowerment. The most cynical interpretation would be that, in order for masculinity to remain hegemonic, it must admit the feminine at certain historical moments.

The new man and similar phenomena are public promotions of a more acceptable and appealing version of masculinity. There are other less confident or positive signs that masculinity has changed, or is believed by men to have changed. David Savran traces the genesis of what he terms 'white male paranoia' to anxieties of the mid-1970s, resulting from five discrete events: the re-emergence of the feminist movement; the limited success of the civil rights movement in relation to affirmative action legislation; the rise of gay and lesbian rights movements; the defeat of the Vietnam War; the end of the post-World War II economic boom (Savran, 1996, p. 128). Particular urgency is given to his depiction of 'white male paranoia' by 1993, when it is widely acknowledged as existent in the United States. The close relationship formed between the popular concept of white male as victim and the paramilitary Right, becomes a matter of wide press discussion in the wake of the Oklahoma City bombing. It is possible to see in such an outcome a reverse of the feminist theme of the personal as political, so that the complexities of political and socio-economic change are made personal.

MASCULINE POWER'S LOSS OF CREDIBILITY

What Savran's paranoid white male has done – to take personally changes within capitalism, for example – may have as part of its appeal a reassuringly simplistic explanation for the sense of victimization, widespread, according to his account, since the 1970s. It may be too difficult to conceptualize, but even more difficult to organize against, a shift within capitalism whereby the power that once rested in individual hands is removed to institutions. Power may remain masculine under that arrangement, but it does not feel that way. Individual males feel passed over. They try to take a dominant role within the public sphere, but even within that role experience a sense of powerlessness.

Something similar might be said of patriarchy's effect on the believability of male power. Patriarchal power, like capitalistic power, is increasingly removed from personal control. Harry Brod, for example, believes that the control exercised over women is men's, but that it is *collective* control. Both men and women are, in his account, increasingly dominated by collective patriarchal powers (Hearn and Morgan (eds),

1990, p. 132). And collective power feels impersonal, no longer in control of the individual male.

IN CONCLUSION

This chapter's exploration of masculinity suggests that there is a disparity between the theory and practice of it. In theory, it is free of the femininity that is equated with weakness, passivity, subordination. In theory, that sort of femininity belongs to women, or else to those men denigrated within masculine ideology. The fantasy males embodied by musclemen stars or by actual, but idolized, sportsmen are an attempt to make the theoretical flesh. And yet they would not be fantasies, objects of worship, if the majority of men in society lived out the masculine ideal.

Practice demands that we think of masculinities as plural. Masculine ideals are summed up in the term 'hegemonic masculinity', but even that cultural ideal seems to change and pluralize as the culture itself changes and fragments with the march of history. Recently, for example, perhaps to protect itself from onslaughts from feminism, hegemonic masculinity has incorporated the feminine. It may have formerly thought of itself as separate from the feminine, but its very hegemony (ascendancy, leadership) has been under threat in the last three decades of the twentieth century precisely because of the exposure of its tactics for holding on to power. One of these tactics was its posture of distancing itself from the femininity of women and the effeminacy of certain men. To continue to hold on to power, the tactics have had to change, even if those tactics must include an admission of vulnerability, sensitivity – in other words, femininity.

It is probably a mistake to see theory and practice as distinct phenomena in this regard. Mass media play a particularly important role in creating the fantasies of 'hegemonic masculinity'. Men's (and to a different extent women's) social behaviour is deeply influenced by common-sense beliefs about and fantasies of masculinity.

The bulk of this book will consider the role of certain mass media, particularly in the creation of notions of masculinity to represent men, after it has considered questions of representation and spectatorship in general. First, though, it will consider what has been achieved for men and suggested about them by men's studies in the 1990s.

Chapter Two

Men's studies and the 'men's movement'

Without feminism, it is unlikely that there would have been 'men's movements' or an academic discipline called 'men's studies'.

Arguably, however, the former grew out of a misunderstanding of feminism and out of what is, in any case, a remarkably common cultural confusion between 'masculine/feminine' and 'man/woman'. The basic aim of feminism is to combat the oppression of women. In order to do this, feminism has analysed the domination of women by men within patriarchy. Anti-feminist men tend to group together under the umbrella of men's movements against what they believe to be feminism's attempt to suppress masculinity.

On the other hand, it is broadly true that men's studies is largely the creation of pro-feminist males. Fred Fejes, for example, discerned men's studies as sharing or adapting the following feminist characteristics: the assumption that gender is a central organizing category of society; the belief that gender, not excepting masculinity, is a social and cultural, not a biological, phenomenon; rejection of the perspective of the male sex role, traditional in social science research (Fejes, 1989, p. 216).

In the 1970s, another reaction to issues about men raised by the Women's Liberation movement late in the previous decade was to reinterpret these issues as matters calling for therapy. Adapting practices from liberal feminism, men's groups concerned themselves with 'consciousness-raising' and critiques of the traditional male role. The therapies were conceived variously: they could involve such diverse approaches as those of herbal medicine, 'Eastern' religion, Jungian psychology, massage, martial arts, New Age mythologies.

Men's studies and men's groups thus have a common source. Yet, therapists concerned with the groups began to claim that their initial pro-feminism meant that something was lacking in their practices. This lack was identified with a sense of the disappearance of masculine feelings. The main thrust of masculinity therapy in the 1980s accordingly became to restore a masculinity believed to have been jettisoned or damaged under the influence of feminists. This shift produced a discernible anti-feminism in men's groups. Noticeable, too, is their unconcern with gay studies and the gay men politicized by it. (Instead, gay studies has its own journals and conferences, largely separate from both men's studies and so-called men's movements.) In the 1970s, moreover, men's groups focused unhesitatingly on male heterosexuality, because they saw sexual and gendered identity as totally separate.

THE PERSPECTIVES OF MEN'S STUDIES

Two of the major issues that have evolved within the perspective of men's studies have been identified by Fred Fejes as male victimization (where men are conceived as passive victims of impersonal socializing forces) and gay male sexuality (which has thrown into question the gender system and traditional notions of masculinity) (Fejes, 1989, p. 216).

Critics of 'the new men's studies' wonder if its creation finally amounts to just another attempt to re-secure male dominance in a new guise. They suspect the very choice of name, since it suggests that these studies of men are complementary to those of women. The complementarity suggested by the name masks the possible result, whereby power is snatched back from the less powerful in the interests of male dominance. Joyce E. Canaan and Christine Griffin ask, 'If men are interested in doing work which is critical of dominant forms of masculinity, why do their main political priorities so seldom involve challenging the patriarchal ... power bases in their own particular fields of work?' These commentators are particularly suspicious of the lack of risk to their careers for teachers of men's studies. Why do they offer no challenge to those men who police the boundaries of academic disciplines and control the budgets for teaching and research? (Joyce E. Canaan and Christine Griffin, in Hearn and Morgan (eds), 1990, pp. 212–213).

The academic study of masculinity has experienced the same surge of popularity which men's studies has enjoyed since the mid-1980s. There could still be a differentiation between the two. Film theory, for example, has taken up the challenge from the comparative lack of theorizations about representations of masculinity in movies. This is not of paramount concern within the curricula of many men's studies programmes, however.

THE MEN'S MOVEMENT IN THE 1990s

Susan Jeffords, in 1993, identifies the philosopher Harry Brod and the sociologist Michael Kimmel, in addition to Robert Bly (whose contribution will be discussed more fully below), as key figures in the men's movement of the 1990s. She also recognises the importance to it of returned Vietnam veterans (Susan Jeffords, in Radher and Collins (eds), 1993, p. 196).

Kimmel and Kaufman, in the course of offering an account of the 'weekend warriors' who largely make up the 'new men's movement' identified by these authors, produce some interesting statistics: the majority of the warriors are between 40 and 55 years of age, with a bias towards the economically privileged, since men of professional, managerial level are most fully represented; only 0–2 per cent are men of colour, only 5 per cent identified as homosexual (Michael S. Kimmel and Michael Kaufman, in Brod and Kaufman (eds), 1994, p. 263).

The main focus appears to be on the healing of wounds believed to have been inflicted on heterosexual men by gender relations. Less sympathetically, the weekend retreats of the men's movement, seeking to rediscover 'emotional masculinity', could be taken to constitute a stand by men against the weakening of their gender privileges.

ROBERT BLY AND 'IRON JOHN'

The poet Robert Bly's publication *Iron John* has easily demonstrable relevance to American men's pursuit in the 1990s of what was believed to be a lost masculinity. For more than 35 weeks in 1991, *Iron John*, published the previous year, topped the bestseller lists. It seemed to offer men a focus for their sense of loss. They now had to learn to 'heal their father wounds' (see below), to rediscover and retrieve the 'warrior within'. Therapists accordingly offered workshops and 'retreats' through which men could undertake their 'gender journey'.

In *Iron John*, Bly argues that men have been unfairly blamed by feminism and that they should thus learn to resist accusations inspired by it. Instead of feeling guilty, men should acknowledge their difference from women and positively celebrate it. His particular emphasis is on the so-called 'father wound' – the emotional damage done to men by separation from their fathers during the Industrial Revolution. The answer is for men to forget about renegotiating their relationships with women and instead to seek a return to forgotten masculinity. Male initiation ritual, he believes, involves separation from the world of women and a rebirth into that of men.

For Bly, manhood is an essence. That is, it is not affected by history, and is shared by, or at least buried within, all males, regardless of their different cultures. Womanhood is also an essence. The difference between men and women is thus, for him, profound and probably unbridgeable, since it is generated by biological sex.

Kimmel and Kaufman define the foundations of Bly's argument under three headings:

1 a psychological analysis of Jungian archetypes, illustrated by fairy tales and myths;
2 a historical interpretation of the effects of industrialization and modernization on men's lives;
3 an anthropological survey of non-industrial cultures and their male inititation rituals.

(Michael S. Kimmel and Michael Kaufman, in Brod and Kaufman (eds), 1994, p. 264)

These three areas deserve further comment. Firstly, the psychologist Carl Jung believed that masculinity contains a degree of femininity. He used Latin labels to clarify this distinction: *animus* for the masculine principle, *anima* for the feminine. Masculinity was explained by him as resulting from the repression of femininity. The *animus/anima* duo was presented in terms of eternal truths about the human psyche, explained by him through a theory of archetypes.

Most of Bly's myths and archetypal figures are found in tales from the Brothers Grimm. He liberally mixes with these further ideas about 'Zeus energy' and other borrowings from oral cultures (cultures in which folktales are transmitted by word of mouth rather than in relatively fixed, literary form). Possibly encouraged by the belief that he is dealing with universal archetypes above cultural specificity, he spends no time on the cultural context from which these archetypal figures are drawn.

Secondly, the damage to manhood which Bly traces from the Industrial Revolution becomes for him unmissable since the 1950s. He dates the increasing power of women from that decade. This is used then to explain the 'diminishment and belittlement of the father', a decline which is traced back and linked up with the killing of kings. Because the father disappears as a model for the son's guidance, the latter turns to the mother for help, but 'only men can change the boy to a man' (Robert Bly, in Jeffords, 1994, p. 9). Without that help, boys run the risk of becoming the next generation of 'soft' men.

Finally, as part of the process whereby Bly turns away from the damaged father whose decline is located within industrialized society, he looks for cultures where the 'wild man' within may be found. Black African bodies are believed by him to offer a place for what he terms the 'deep masculine'. David Savran believes, on this evidence, that Bly's so-called 'mythopoetics' are firmly rooted in imperialistic fantasies (Savran, 1996, p. 141). These could be illustrated by the concept of the 'noble savage'.

The domesticity created for weekend warriors, away from the family as much as from the office, is reminiscent of a teepee space. 'Home' is a place created by and for men, where lost intimacy between fathers and sons may be rediscovered.

There are obvious problems with both the diagnosis and the cure offered by Robert Bly. Most obvious of all is his belief that being born biologically male is a sufficient explanation for masculinity, which is, after all, a gender term. Gender in the view of social science is a product of human action. Conceptions of masculinity result from discourse and social struggle. Bly's essentialism allows him to pin the responsibility for the decline of his version of masculinity on feminism or, more simply, on women who claim power for themselves. This means that he can avoid consideration of the historical and political analyses through which reasons for the loss of masculine power might better be grasped.

Then, again, his belief that a fuller, better masculinity can be retrieved by means of separation from the world of women needs more careful thought. Manhood is frequently explained – and, significantly, seems to be so understood by Jung – as involving flight from and repression of the feminine within the male subject. Male fear of attitudes that are culturally linked with the feminine means that men have to do battle with themselves over matters of affection, dependency, compassion. It could surely be suggested that the cure is not likely to be found in still more separation from the mother during the early period of the male child's socialization. Notably in this regard, Bly is inspired by inititation rituals practised in cultures where women's status is at its lowest.

IN CONCLUSION

The emergence of men's studies as part of the university curriculum, the suddenly increased interest within film studies in the representation of masculinity, the burgeoning of weekend retreats and other manifestations of men's movements inspired by John Bly, can be viewed as separate phenomena. The profound distrust of essentialism in the majority of Higher Education's considerations of gender is enough, on its own, to distinguish these academic endeavours from movements that conceive of the 'deep masculine' as something eternal, though for the moment hidden and devalued. Indeed, much of the academic interest in representations of masculinity is inspired by a fresh awareness that masculinity is a gender, not a biological given, that it thus shifts in accordance with social and political change and that it requires deconstruction of the sort that feminism has, since the 1970s, given to images of women. There could hardly be a clearer sign of how anti-academic, in this particular sense, the men's movement based on Bly is. Middle-class white men go off on weekend retreats with other men, believing that what they will discover on these is a form of 'the eternal masculine', threatened by industrialization, nearly extinguished by at least four decades of feminism, but waiting hidden to reinvigorate itself and leap into life.

Nevertheless, what these objects of study and this public concern with manhood strongly suggest in combination is that masculinity must surely have become destabilized. Where it once was taken for granted as transparent, normal, too natural to require explanation, it has become something of an enigma. A masculinity which takes up so much energy and demands so much attention is self-evidently unconfident about its nature and attributes. Masculinity is, not for the first time, in crisis.

Chapter Three

Representation and spectatorship

The two areas covered in this chapter are discussed here in general terms. These wider areas – of representation and spectatorship in general – are, however, important for our understanding of the particular matter of men's representation before we proceed, in Part B, to specific examples of this representation in mass media.

First, representation itself is considered in at least two respects: why both it and its field, popular culture, are so important for the creation and perpetuation of the 'common sense' of masculinity; what sort of work has been done on this by academics and what value we may place on this work.

Secondly, because work on the content of popular representation does not usually tell us *how* it is received and assimilated by popular audiences, this chapter asks whether certain ways of seeing and understanding are built into mass media, as it were. Film studies has a particular contribution to make in this regard, in that it has generated a lengthy and influential debate about the role of gender in cinema viewing. Does this debate inform us only of spectatorship within the peculiar conditions of cinema-going, or can it be broadened to offer directions for viewing of other media?

THE IMPORTANCE OF POPULAR REPRESENTATION

The way we think about gender, and about so many other features of our lives, is both reflected in and produced by the images that surround us in our culture. Popular conceptions are vitally concerned with popular culture.

Groups that are marginalized in real life thus feel concern about stereotyping in popular media representations. These groups usually try to influence producers of popular culture to question the stereotypes about them in entertainment. The belief of the groups is that multiple and diverse portrayals can inspire new thinking about politically and socially disadvantaged categories of people. Without this sort of questioning of content and images, it is feared that popular culture feeds rather than challenges stereotypes. Dominant attitudes not only dominate, but 'normalize'. Thus, what dominant groups see is all that is allowed to be seen. It soon becomes the only way to see. Particular versions become, by this process, 'universal' and 'natural'. Political and social life stagnates.

This may be why, in early studies of mass culture, media were assumed to be inferior and illiterate, not worthy of serious analysis. If mass culture was thought to be deadeningly homogenized, culture critics themselves were also homogenized. They were largely white, middle class and highly educated. Yet, this particular example of homogenization was little noticed by them.

METHODOLOGIES FOR ANALYSING POPULAR REPRESENTATION

It has become commonplace to notice that there are many contradictions between life as shown in the media ('mediated') and the lives lived by the majority of citizens, not only of the socially marginalized. Content analyses on their own can tell us disappointingly little of the society that popular culture is assumed to relate to. Representation does not merely reflect. It does not neutrally transmit a pre-existing meaning. It is more likely to provide a meaning that it has created. In Michael Kimmel's words, media representations 'tell us who we are, who we should be, and who we should avoid' (Michael S. Kimmel, in Craig (ed.), 1992, p. xii).

Yet, all media texts need not be understood, 'read', in a uniform manner. Rather than think of audiences as passive consumers of media images, we should be aware of the possibility or even the likelihood of multiple 'readings' which could include a resistant variety. Stuart Hall goes so far as to suggest that there is 'no necessary correspondence' between a television message 'encoded' by its producer and the message that is 'decoded' by the viewer (Stuart Hall, in Gallagher, 1992, p. 4). The viewer's decoding could theoretically be classified as 'dominant-hegemonic' when it is in line with the common sense of dominant groups in society. It could also, though, be 'negotiated' or even 'oppositional'.

This awareness that readings may be so unpredictable as to be turned back against the encoder, helps to make sense of what could otherwise be puzzling questions: why mass culture, which helps to oppress politically and socially marginalized groups, can be so appealing to, and so obviously enjoyed by, members of these same groups; why Hollywood, whose images of women are believed by feminism to be so damaging to women's interests, is so unexpectedly fascinating to feminists; why the media may be argued to be more important to homosexual identity and socialization than to the heterosexual counterparts.

Nevertheless, if it is too pessimistic to see viewers as passive, undiscerning consumers of meanings encoded elsewhere, it is surely over-optimistic to believe that they are 'free' to choose from a variety of potential meanings. Hall draws back from that position when, in 1980, he cautions, 'If there were no limits, audiences could simply read whatever they liked into any message' (Stuart Hall, in Gallagher, 1992, p. 13). There are likely and less likely interpretations. All the same, some commentators are reluctant to soft-pedal the importance of the notion of popular culture as a site of contest. Andrew Ross, for example, conceives of popular culture as 'a medium in which ideological consent is either won or lost' (Andrew Ross, in Grossberg and Treichler, 1987, p. 284). If that is so, then victory is not a foregone conclusion: 'The stakes are real, the outcome uncertain, and our role as critics more vital than ever' (Grossberg and Treichler, 1987, p. 286).

The discussion so far has been noticeably theoretical, suggesting logically appealing probabilities. This sort of theorization calls out for another sort. It needs to be backed, if not exactly replaced, by *empirical* research, that is, research into the facts of viewing.

The focus of empirical research has often been on children. Suggestive as this sort of research may be, it cannot hope to come up with definitive answers about media influences. All such research is dogged by the extreme difficulty of separating out media effects from effects in general. For instance, it is surely not enough to explore in isolation the possible correlation between antisocial aggressive behaviour in children and a film that they have watched whose message could be considered antisocial and aggressive. Why are some children more prone to aggression than others? What part do class and gender play (for instance, boys are normally thought to be more aggressive than girls)? What sort of family life have these children experienced? Media influence is but one possible factor, albeit an important one.

Feminists, particularly in the 1980s, felt a great deal of concern about the social effects of pornography in general and about violent pornography in particular, as well as about sexually violent images in mass media. Whether coincidentally or not, the latter were believed to have increased in the 1970s but then to become less frequent in the 1980s. It might be worth citing the findings of one piece of empirical research, to illustrate its relevance to such concern.

It was concluded of a student experiment that viewing sexually aggressive films and violent primetime television augmented male, but not female, acceptance of interpersonal violence. It also seemed to increase male openness to rape myth – that women who say no are really saying yes, for example. In 1983, Malamuth and Check deduced, however, that the sexual or pornographic context was a red herring. They concluded that viewing of 'sex-only' films did not increase male propensity to violence or to acceptance of rape mythology. On the other hand, 'violence-only' viewing did. They suggested, too, that if sexual violence can be learned by exposure to certain viewing material, it can surely also be 'unlearned'. Donnerstein and Linz, reporting these findings, ask, 'Are the media, and in particular pornography, the cause?' and report, 'If anything, the media act to reinforce already existing attitudes and values regarding women and violence. They do contribute, but are only part of the problem' (Edward Donnerstein and Daniel Linz, in Kimmel (ed.), 1987, p. 212).

This sort of experiment would suggest that empirical research can be a valuable method of testing a widely respected hypothesis. The result though, as here, is often, to undermine over-confidence in the hypothesis rather than to produce certainty of its own.

Empirical work on media representations of men originally tended to use the methods of traditional content analysis. Particular attention was given to the extent to which media content, especially that of television, involved stereotypical male sex roles. Thus, notice was taken of the number of male characters in a programme in relation to female, the status and conditions of their employment, their characterization as rational, intelligent, more active, and so on. A further area of research has been the effect of sex-role stereotypes in media on viewers, in particular on young male viewers. A major problem with more traditional content analysis is that its frequent work of juxtaposing 'positive' and 'negative' images, or stereotypical and anti-stereotypical images, assumes a norm against which these classifications can be made.

Fejes believes that a major drawback in these approaches is that this research does not focus on masculinity itself, and that it is based on a traditional analysis of 'manifest content' (that is, that it does not dig beneath the surface of what is shown). Masculinity, Fejes contends, shows great variation in terms of class, time period, ethnic group. Therefore, the meanings to be drawn from media depictions of men should be expected likewise to show great variation. Instead, a particular conception of masculinity – that of white, heterosexual, middle-class Americans – is used as the basis for much research into media masculinity (Fejes, 1989, p. 217). Fejes recommends a 'semiotic' approach as a corrective to these tendencies. The point of this is that semiotics (the study of 'signs' and thus of signification/meaning) would foreground masculinity as a social construct and as, in that sense, an artificial product (Fejes, 1989, p. 218). It would involve more scepticism. Rather than assuming that masculinity was already there to be discerned in terms of stereotyping or questioning of stereotyping, the semiotic approach makes few assumptions about its depiction. Instead, it notes how masculinity is constructed within particular programmes, rather than how these programmes' depiction confirms or undermines an already existent version of masculinity.

Earlier content analyses have more recently been replaced with a desire to explore the relationship between texts and cultural struggles. Gender has been placed at the centre of cultural contestation. The focus on masculinity has been made possible by the replacement of an approach which treated masculinity as a fact, with another, which explores the facticity (the constructedness) of masculinity.

This needs to be supplemented by consideration of the role that gender may play in the way that men and women view media and see the world.

GENDERED SPECTATORSHIP

The most frequently cited and reprinted article in the short history of film studies is almost certainly 'Visual Pleasure and Narrative Cinema'. This was written by the feminist film studies scholar, Laura Mulvey, and published by *Screen* in 1975 (Mulvey, 1989, pp. 14–26). Some of its principal ideas need to be grasped, not only because they broke new ground at the time of this publication, but because they were largely agreed with and assented to far beyond their original context. Any account of spectatorship needs now to discuss gender because Mulvey's ideas proved so influential. Any such account which does not acknowledge and deal with her contribution seems inadequate.

She argues that 'the cinematic apparatus' involves three looks (viewpoints): that of the camera at what was originally filmed; that of characters within the movie at each other (so labelled 'diegetic looking', 'diegetic' being a term for that which is contained within the world of a movie narrative); and that of the spectator.

The most popular example of narrative cinema in the Western world is what Hollywood makes and exports. Hollywood takes great pains, Mulvey points out, to make the spectator unaware of that particular look. Instead, the spectator, by identifying strongly with the hero, the male protagonist of the narrative, looks through his eyes, as it were. Mulvey argues that the female in classic Hollywood cinema (during the period of the studios and the heyday of the studio system) is always an erotic object for the hero. Her whole function is what Mulvey terms 'to-be-looked-at-ness'. Because she is objectified by the hero's look, she is made available as an erotic object for the spectator's look. Yet, the cinema spectator is spared 'responsibility' for her objectification, because of the psychological closeness felt with the hero.

This argument about the powerful presence and seemingly paradoxical invisibility of the spectator's look at the female object is underpinned by psychoanalysis. Making use – some would assert too uncritical and free use – of the ideas of Sigmund Freud and Jacques Lacan, Mulvey links the psychoanalytic concept of 'castration anxiety' to her version of spectatorial visual pleasure. She uses it to explain the sheltering of the cinema spectator from realization of what the spectator's look amounts to.

Castration anxiety, according to Freud, is a fear that is aroused by the sight of female genitals. The child, glimpsing his mother's nakedness, interprets her genital difference as a sign that she lacks that which he has. If this can be removed from her, could it not likewise be removed from him? In other words, he fears castration. (The comment should be made at this point that it is unlikely that this interpretation and this fear could be conceptualized as neatly in a young infant as Freud suggests.)

Erotic pleasure, which is what visual pleasure comes close to amounting to in Mulvey, is always accompanied by castration fear. The brilliant achievement of popular cinema, in her account, is that it spares the spectator awareness that the female, whose objectification apparently guarantees erotic viewing pleasure, has been made into an object for the cinema spectator's pleasure. Surely, it seems, it is the on-screen hero who brings her objectification about. In a sense, the spectator is merely following the story, making sense of the narrative, which happens to centre on, for example, the hero's erotic conquest of the heroine.

We should be aware of certain facets of this account, so briefly and perhaps inadequately summarized above. In particular, the spectator does not seem to be an actual human being, so much as a 'position', created by the text. This sort of spectatorship is apparatic, rather than actual. It is the sort of spectatorship made possible and offered to viewers by the cinematic apparatus – which includes the camera, the projector, the darkness. That darkness is necessitated by projection, but it increases the sense of peeping into an illuminated world, much as a peeping Tom is drawn to the lighted window of a house at night.

Feminist and other readers, impressed by this account, nevertheless asked of it why a feminist writer would always refer to the spectator by the pronoun 'he'. What about the woman in the audience? Because Mulvey chose to answer this question in the way that she did, in her 'Afterthoughts' paper of 1981 (Mulvey, 1989, pp. 29–38), the ground had surely shifted by this point. How could the text-created spectator of her 'Visual Pleasure' article continue to be thought about as a position, rather than a person, when it had been personalized by the 'woman in the audience' question?

What she illuminates in 1981 is that the spectator of her 1975 account is at least a masculine position if not an actual male. The visual pleasure created for this spectator caters to (heterosexual) male desires. Castration anxiety concerns male fear. Diminution of it in erotic contemplation of the female object through the hero's eyes is of advantage to a socially male spectator. The female viewer under the spell of a narrative movie can be so only if she too is viewing through the hero's eyes and identifying with masculine pleasures (and avoiding masculine anxieties). Either she is happy with the temporary fantasy of 'masculinization' or she oscillates between identification and a more distanced psychological viewing position. Mulvey ends her 1981 paper by pointing out the instability of a female viewing position which boils down to pretending to be a man or to think and feel like a man in society: 'the female spectator's fantasy of masculinization [is] at cross-purposes with itself, restless in its transvestite clothes' (Mulvey, 1989, p. 37).

If there is a female spectator, not just an ideal or apparatic spectator position, then there must surely be a male spectator. If the female spectator is restless in transvestite garb, then presumably the male occupies a spectator position which delights him and protects him from anxiety. He can wear the clothes of his own gender, and with far less investment in fantasy can project himself psychologically into the male hero and share in his victory over the desired woman.

Mulvey's account owes much of its considerable influence to the way it shows a world of sexual imbalance, a world where the male is the subject, active and dominating, and the female is the object, passive and dominated. It owes still more to the way it shows the cinema responding to and, as it were, strengthening that gender imbalance.

In the more than two decades that have passed since Mulvey first offered her thoughts and afterthoughts on visual pleasure, dissent has become more vocal.

One objection is that the Gaze discussed by Jacques Lacan is transcendental (hence, the capital 'g'). That is, it does not belong to, and cannot be within the power of, either gender. When the gaze of cinema viewing is taken by Mulvey as 'a male gaze', then men assert gazing power over female objects by a kind of imposture. They have seized what is not rightfully theirs and stuck a label on the stolen property as if it had passed into their ownership.

There is a less abstruse and more far-reaching criticism of Mulvey's version of Hollywood, where only females are to-be-looked-at and only males do the looking. Is it really the case that male stars are never erotic objects?

We were used to cinema fare in the 1980s where the 'spectacular bodies' represented by the likes of Arnold Schwarzenegger, Sylvester Stallone and Jean-Claude Van Damme invited our viewing attention. These bodies may be entirely naked, albeit in long-shot for frontal nudity and with closer scrutiny permitted to their rears. They are the bodies, naked or clothed, of men performing herculean tasks. These men therefore seem so active and dominating that their subject status looks as if it is never in doubt. Yet, we *are* looking at them, since they are on the cinema screen, and we are looking at them intently, because they are movie heroes. The narrative even pauses to give us time to contemplate them, as we do, according to Mulvey, female objects.

Perhaps the answer is once again that we are allowed by this sort of cinema not to take responsibility for our gaze. Men can shift it on to the female spectator and her presumed desires – or else to homosexual males, from whom 'real men' take pains to distance themselves psychologically. We may be in the presence of disavowal. That is, something which is manifestly happening is disavowed, treated as if it were not happening – or treated with a different significance to that which it seems to have.

Take, for example, the male star of the classic western who strips away his shirt when he is wounded by an arrow in his chest. (Usually, there is a woman present in the scene, who tends him with a piece of clothing dipped in cool water.) He has taken his shirt off, not to give visual pleasure, but because he is, according to the narrative, bleeding and requires the wound to be tended uninterrupted by this item of clothing. If the male in the audience beholds the bare-chested male star as being in some way erotic, then an explanation is provided. His eroticization is in spite of the common sense of the narrative and perhaps because the female on screen or others in the audience are looking at him that way.

In 1992's *Universal Soldier*, Jean-Claude Van Damme strips completely naked (except for his white socks!) in a motel bedroom and then stands naked outside it in the presence of one attractive female and in the sight of a (lascivious) old lady. The strip is not 'for' them in narrative terms. The character played by Van Damme is as innocent as a baby. In the narrative, he is no exhibitionist, because he has not yet developed human emotions, being a 'Unisol', a fighting machine created by science from his dead self. If we become aware of staring at the naked star, we can remind ourselves that we are just following the story – when the Unisol's body heats up dangerously, it has to be cooled by the removal of clothes before an ice bath can be arranged. If there is an erotic element, it seems definitely not to be willed by the hero. The young female is embarrassed, while the older one licks her lips in appreciation. The latter surely cannot be our identification figure – for one thing, we know almost nothing about her and she plays such a brief part in the story – while the former's social discomfort permits the spectator an 'out' for any perception of eroticism in the nudity. It isn't *meant* to be erotic. If anybody takes it that way within the narrative, it is through a comic misunderstanding or exploitation of the hero's plight.

Nudity, male nudity in particular, has become much more frequent since the classic period of Hollywood. Yet, hasn't it always been the case that male stars are looked at? That look is surely recognized, in an up-front way, as erotic in the case of silent-screen star Rudolph Valentino, or rock stars such as Elvis Presley and Cliff Richard on film in the later 1950s. The spectator may believe that the look is about viewer location of and identification with the hero in his adventures. The one who looks on screen at the hero is likely to be female if the look is erotic, so that fears of homoeroticism are not aroused. What this shows, though, is the massive investment in disavowal by popular cinema, rather than that the gazed-upon hero is always the subject, never the eroticized object.

Gender plays an important role even in this different account of spectatorship, concerned with looking at a male rather than female object. The erotic look at the female star is without alibi, overt and even blatant, because the more the female is objectified, the more masculinity seems to be guaranteed to the hero – and thus, to follow Mulvey's logic, to the male spectator. The look at the male star is heavily alibied, covert, confusing, its erotic qualities projected on to females and, occasionally, gay males. It is surely no coincidence that hegemonic masculinity seems to feel most threatened by these categories of people. Cinema does indeed seem to protect its male spectators in particular from feeling responsible for eroticizing the look at the female. However, this protection is extremely simple when compared to the inventive range of protection it gives to its male spectators in particular for looking at the male in a sexual or erotic manner. Masculinity is shored up, and all threat of homoeroticism and feminization kept at bay.

MASCULINIZATION OF THE FEMALE SPECTATOR/ FEMINIZATION OF THE MALE SPECTATOR?

As noted above, Laura Mulvey characterizes the visual pleasure of cinematic looking as 'male'. The female spectator, she explains in 1981, can gain access to this pleasure only by a process of psychological transvestism, by which she is, in effect, 'masculinized'.

By this understanding, the cinema audience which enjoys a Hollywood narrative movie is made up of men and women who are sufficiently 'masculinized' as to be virtually men. Both sexes have as their identification point the male protagonist of the movie.

This suggests that classic Hollywood provides a remarkably masculine experience, offering to the audience as a whole what amount to male pleasures of fantasized activity and dominance. Once the eroticized male object is recognized as part of the pleasure on offer, the situation in the cinema surely changes. What happens when the masculine hero is put on show and becomes to-be-looked-at? Presumably, his objectification at that point is not only heavily disavowed, but temporary. It suspends his activity and dominance for a short period.

So, what happens in that short period to what seems, in Mulvey, to be the audience's unbroken identification with the active hero? If he is looked at, and thus becomes passive, does identification with him cease, to be taken up again only when he is restored to activity and dominance? Alternatively, does identification with him in his objectified moments mean that the audience identifies with him in his passive, and therefore feminized, state? Does the male spectator thus undergo feminization just as the female spectator is thought to undergo masculinization in order to take pleasure in a classic movie? This feminization may be hidden from the spectator. In any case, it is as alibied and disavowed as the objectification of the male on screen. Nevertheless, one way of understanding the uneasiness summoned up by identification with a feminized hero is to adapt Mulvey's consideration of the female spectator – perhaps the male spectator is also 'restless in [his] transvestite clothes'.

Then, too, maybe feminization – of the male spectator and his identification figure, the male protagonist – may be a far less temporary phenomenon than just suggested. A point that Mulvey seems not to consider is that just about every Hollywood genre movie involves a love story. In musicals and the genre that Film Studies calls melodrama, love may be at the very centre of the narrative. In war films and westerns, it may be reduced to the point where it is talked of vaguely by critics as 'love interest'. It is omnipresent, part to a greater or lesser extent of all classic Hollywood. This makes omission of consideration of the love story in Mulvey (as in most Film Studies work) worthy of notice. Most of what she says about the active hero's conquest of the heroine is a fair analysis of at least the first half of Hollywood genre movies' running time. In the first part of the movie, the central male and female may 'spar' and even hurl insults at one another. The audience is seldom fooled, though. It expects this pair eventually to admit their attraction to each other, and to form a steady relationship culminating in marriage. This is indeed what usually happens.

Once each half of the couple stops struggling and submits to the desire that they feel for each other, the language of conquest and defeat seems misleading. The man depicted as being in love is no longer the masterful, independent character that he was at the start of the narrative. The gazing between the lovers is less from male subject to helpless female object than it is reciprocal. The woman invites and even

31

returns the gaze. The man may be expected regularly to be gazed at with tenderness or passion by his female beloved.

Roland Barthes' account of 'the lover's discourse' draws attention to the way that being in love regularly feminizes. 'A man is not feminized', he says, 'because he is inverted but because he is in love' (Barthes, 1978, p. 14). In his description of the feelings of love, he emphasizes mutuality rather than mere possession of one by the other: 'I want to possess, fiercely, but I also know how to give, actively' (Barthes, 1978, p. 126). Or, again, he stresses the overpowering gentleness of reciprocated love: 'There is not only need for tenderness, there is also need to be tender for the other; we shut ourselves up in a mutual kindness, we mother each other reciprocally; we return to the root of all relations, where need and desire join' (Barthes, 1978, p. 224).

If the spectator, male and female alike, identifies with the hero, then that identification presumably remains when the hero falls in love and, to follow Barthes' thoughts on the matter, thus becomes feminized. The alternative is that the spectator identifies with the couple in love rather than with two distinct individuals. After all, the woman in love is less an object than she was when the hero fought to win her over. The power differentials between male and female remain, but they have narrowed.

It is possible to go all the way with this idea and to suggest that, if the spectator may identify with a feminized hero or with a male/female couple, it is hard to see what insurmountable barrier there is to his/her identification with a heroine. The male spectator can be so regularly feminized in movie-watching, however secret that process is to him, as to identify with heroes when they are eroticized into objects or feminized by love. If that is so, why, in theory, should he not also be capable of being feminized sufficiently as to identify with a female character? Presumably he must be when he watches a 'woman's picture' of the 1940s, or a woman-centred melodrama such as Douglas Sirk's 1959 *Imitation of Life*. Why not beyond those areas, too, when, for instance, the female character is to some extent 'subjectified' by love?

WHAT ABOUT MEDIA OTHER THAN MOVIES?

Laura Mulvey herself makes very clear that her version of spectatorship relates to the cinematic apparatus. For that reason, there must be considerable caution about transporting the analysis of gendered spectatorship in Mulvey's terms beyond that apparatus.

Movies once made for the cinema are increasingly likely to be viewed today in a domestic space, in the form of video cassettes or DVDs, or when they are shown on television. The context alters the experience of viewing. Visual pleasure may well be differently conceived in the new context for what were once exclusively cinema films.

For one thing, the visual power presumably decreases as the screen diminishes. For another, the placement of the screen demands less attention than the viewer has to give to the cinema screen. The TV screen is viewed in light rather than darkness. To become fully involved with a drama on screen, the television viewer may have to resort to such tactics as leaving telephone calls to an answering machine. Even when this viewer is left alone, interruptions are supplied by advertising breaks on commercial channels. The televisual apparatus is very different in many respects from the cinematic. For that reason alone, gendered spectatorship is likely to differ between cinema and television, for example.

No work to match the energy of the debates about cinema spectatorship has been produced so far for television. As was once the case with cinema, assumptions seem to be made broadly that viewers create personal, subjective readings. Alternatively, a particular model of spectatorship, usually that provided by Mulvey in 1975, is uncritically applied to TV viewing, when that version has been increasingly questioned even within the context of cinema.

Marjorie Kibby and Brigid Costello, on the other hand, have conducted an examination of a far more recent medium, the Internet, in terms of what it seems to say about erotic objectification as it relates to the male (Kibby and Costello, 1999).

They are interested in video-conferencing sites on which men present their own bodies as objects of the gaze. This suggests to them that there is a new sexual discourse available and that interactive pornography destabilizes traditional regimes of pleasure. Now, participants become both subject and object of the gaze, blurring the distinction between consumer and consumed. While the majority of these participants are white American males, there are many women and couples also involved.

Their conclusion is that lived relations of power are subverted by the detached nature of the medium. Cyberspace offers an opportunity to explore and reinterpret sexual identities where activity/passivity and distributions of power had been more clear-cut in actuality. Of this, it could be remarked that by the 1980s, with advertising and movies often featuring male erotic objects, and with the success of the Chippendales and more 'full-Monty' male strip shows, male sexual identity was already visibly altering. Perhaps, the newness was more apparent than real, in that gender's relation with erotic objectification is much more tangled, as suggested above, than it would appear to be in Mulvey's account. Interactive sites in which men choose to put themselves on display are the newest and most explicit of the apparently new media demonstrations of the blurring of subject and object, active and passive.

IN CONCLUSION

The wide-ranging arguments of this chapter suggest, for a start, that totting up portrayals of men to form conclusions about masculinity's representation in popular media does not take the student of gender very far. That sort of content analysis assumes that masculinity is already known as a stable concept in actuality. It might be more helpful to find how masculinity is constructed by various programmes in various media and then 'sold' to viewers. It is because masculinity is so unstable as a concept in social actuality that it has to be constructed and reconstructed repeatedly in the mass media.

Traditional content analysis falls down in another major fashion. Its assumption seems to be that the object viewed tells us all that we need to know of the meaning placed upon that object, and that viewing itself is neutral in effect, as well as invisible. Film Studies of the 1970s and 1980s make it difficult to go on believing that viewing is a neutral activity on which no analytic care needs to be expended. What was probably an initial strength of Laura Mulvey's 'Visual Pleasure and Narrative Cinema' was the clarity of its distinctions between subject and object, viewer and viewed, looker and looked at, and then, in 1981, the clarity with which the male and female spectator seemed to emerge. In the 1990s, in particular, those clear-cut distinctions may seem to be the principal weakness of this seminal article. The credibility of the separateness of male and female spectatorship, the instability of subject and object sexual positions, are re-explored in that decade. By today, with the additional evidence of interactive pornographic Internet sites to go on, it is far more difficult to maintain that the common-sense social gender of spectators can safely be used to predict psychological positioning in terms of the erotic.

While gender and spectatorship have a great deal to do with each other, that relationship is now far from easy to describe confidently. After all, the context in which the relationship has to be explored is that of media texts, with their own difficulties of interpretation in relation to life. Furthermore, the particular context within that context is erotic fantasy, where common sense seems least easy to apply.

Part B

Representation in Specific Media

Chapter Four
Masculinity in movies

The movie industry has, for much of the last century, been a key source for images of dominant masculinity. An obvious illustration of this is the way that the films of Arnold Schwarzenegger, Sylvester Stallone and Bruce Willis became so successful at the box office from the late 1970s far into the 1980s. The stress in these movies on physical size, strength and the ability to use violence effectively suggested that masculine identity was being linked with the use of the body as an instrument of power and control, and that viewers liked that link. Perhaps masculinity in society was once again in crisis, reeling from women's challenges to male domination and gains by people of colour – gains which were taken by some to be at the expense of the white working class.

The bulk of this chapter will consider a wide variety of movie genres, individual movies and male stars. The potential evidence is so much more widespread and vast, though, that concentration will largely be on the work that *has* been done on masculinity and movies rather than the almost endless possibilities of what might be done. The hope is that an examination of this evidence will suggest the array of methods through which movie images of masculinity have helped Western culture to construct notions of masculine identity, and also how wide-ranging these images can be.

GENRES

The easily recognizable generic categories of classic Hollywood covered such sets of films as westerns, war movies and comedies, for example. They would not have included more modern sets such as 'the male-paranoia movie', for example. Technically, too, the slasher movie is more of a sub-genre of the horror movie genre than a genre in its own right. Nevertheless, the genre heading is used, not always too precisely, to group together what seem to be different types of movies with particular relevance – according to those who have devoted attention to them – to the study of masculinity.

THE ACTION GENRE

The huge commercial success of *Star Wars* in 1977 and *Raiders of the Lost Ark* in 1981 opened the door to investment in the production of action movies. Whether this was coincidental or not, a version of heroism was promoted in these movies that depended on visual evidence of physical strength and might. Top-grossing movies in the 1980s and for a little time thereafter were of the action genre, but with superior production values, ostentatiously showing off the elaboration of their special effects, especially in scenes of destruction. These top grossers included the two *Terminator* movies, and the *Rambo, Die Hard* and *Batman* franchises.

The most highly paid stars were those associated with action – such stars as Arnold Schwarzenegger, Sylvester Stallone and Clint Eastwood. At a lower level of expenditure were action movies starring the likes of Jean-Claude Van Damme or Dolph Lundgren. If these stars seemed to embody superheroes, the characters whom they played were usually not supermen. They were more likely to be everyday guys dealing with everyday problems in extraordinary ways.

John Rambo (Sylvester Stallone) is initially a Vietnam veteran robbed of such authority as he once had. His answer is to 'go native' against the peacetime authorities who, because they fail to understand him, physically abuse him. So-called 'male rampage' movies involve wild men, whose wildness stems from surprising sensitivity. They may suffer anguish over a marriage which is failing or defunct (Mel Gibson in the first *Lethal Weapon*). They are often called on in the course of the narrative to deal with corrupt or criminal authority. To do so, they have to arm themselves, literally and metaphorically, to become fearsome sites of resistance to the evil around them, as well as to the demons within them.

The world of heroes is often homosocial, involving close contact with and dependence on men alone. The perceived risk of homoeroticism is, however, vigorously resisted through insistence on heterosexual romance or marriage – or, more bluntly, by overt homophobia. Relationships with buddies are normally expressed through roughhousing and banter, intimacy kept at bay by male bravado. Action-movie buddies are often reminiscent of schoolboy friends, close in feeling but afraid of that closeness. Bonding with females sometimes seems to have value only from the perspective of approval from other males held dear. If love for family and female partners in romance is demonstrated and supported, that sort of love is less emotionally engaging than the hero's feelings for his sidekick. Some of this could be illustrated with the example of the Mel Gibson/Danny Glover team in *Lethal Weapon*. Gibson is the tortured, sensitive soul and seems to be the stronger audience identification point, while Glover is the fully domesticated character.

Fred Pfeil explains the action genre's relation to social actuality with reference to the *Lethal Weapon* and *Die Hard* films and the warning that they constitute: 'if, as activists and theorists, we find ourselves uninterested in the task of seeking to manage, mind, and redefine th[e] white-straight-working-man sign, other groups and forces will certainly be willing to shoulder the task for us, and in ways we are unlikely to approve' (Pfeil, 1995, p. 33). Seen thus, some of the most commercially successful movies of the 1980s can be understood to be exploring the effects on working men of seismic change in the economy, in relations with women, in the role of technology as regards militarism, of tensions in race relations, of wider tensions brought about by American foreign policy.

The resolution of conflict within the films seems to enshrine the family ideal at a time of rising divorce rates and a decrease in traditional family organization. More widely, it suggests that community ideals promoted in American culture can be revived if only the selfishness involved in the race for power and material wealth is abandoned. The hero of *Blade Runner* (1982) seems to be the last hope for survival of the personal and human in the face of corporate control and manipulation via consumerism. Often, 'the system' is depicted in action movies of this period as colourless and impersonal. Safety is then found in the self and its love of what is to be interpreted as freedom.

BOND MOVIES

In the 1960s, a relatively new set of gendered identities seemed to be offered by James Bond and the 'Bond girl'. The new norm of masculinity represented by Bond could be seen to involve the shaking off of the constraints of gentlemanly chivalry and his extrication from the asexuality or repressed sexuality of the English aristocratic hero. Tony Bennett and Janet Woollacott conclude, in their book-length study of Bond's 'political career', that when Bond is sent on a mission he is symbolically castrated. He is without a gun, or else much is made of the fact that his weaponry is granted to him by and under the orders of M. Occasionally, he is threatened with actual physical castration (Bennett and Woollacott, 1987, p. 134).

Moreover, two decades before Stallone's Rambo, Sean Connery in his incarnation of 007, apart from being unmistakably Scottish, is without doubt the object of the erotic look both within the narrative of the Bond movies and for the audience. His highly qualified masculinity is further compromised as the Bond series moves on. Even in those Bond films where Connery continues to play the hero, technological excess becomes a principal source of pleasure in spectacle for the audience, sidelining the focus on the hero.

RAMBO MOVIES

Former US President Ronald Reagan was quick to grasp the popular appeal of Sylvester Stallone's embodiment of the hypermasculine, phallic John Rambo in relation to a new version of history. This new version was welcomed by a huge public anxious, on one interpretation of the evidence, to overcome the 'psychological castration' of defeat in Vietnam.

What might have been less obvious on a first viewing was the strong link created between Rambo's aggressive masculinity and Nature. To reassert himself, Rambo in *First Blood* withdraws into the forest, where he discards most of his clothing and seems to become one with nature. Pastoralism, preached by Thomas Jefferson and more subtly promoted by the western film genre, according to Paul Budra, is an ideology associated with the Right in this period (Budra, 1990, p. 190). By his retreat into the forest, Rambo most closely resembles, paradoxically, not so much the American fighting man as the Viet Cong.

In his alignment with the natural world, Rambo seems implicitly opposed to the world of modern technology. In his individualism, he seems more human than the unjust, impersonal system that he is fighting. Yet, both these conclusions may be too narrow. Rambo's body is itself a machine. It is as if the salvation for masculinity that he represents demands an integration of nature and technology, the sort of fusion celebrated in *Robocop*. Rather than think of the system as inherently unjust or impersonal, the Rambo movies seem to imagine the possibility of a restored, more humane and ethically refurbished system.

Emotional entanglements with women are carefully contained, so that, as with the hero of westerns, Rambo may stay isolated and able to concentrate on the righting of wrongs with confidence in his individual, masculine powers.

In this sense, and in several others too, masculinity involves an element of paranoia and vigilance against enemies without, but also within (such internal enemies as 'softness' and diversion from a single-minded mission). It involves a sense of victimization. Rambo's violence, in context, is a near-inevitable response to the treacherousness of American authorities. The attractiveness of using this in explanation of the Patriot movement in the 1990s is not lost on David Savran (Savran, 1996, p. 131).

The final images of Rambo, triumphant, with American masculinity restored, may blind the audience to the movie's strong investment in images of suffering and the detail of the hero's pain throughout much of its running time. Audience involvement and empathy with Rambo's suffering suggest an important place for masochism (meaning, to put it simply, pleasure in pain) in the Rambo movies. Of course, it is an important part of the morality of Rambo's violence that it should be provoked by the cruel infliction of pain. However, the detailed rendering of this pain, the loving attention to colour, sound and extreme close-ups is difficult to explain away just in relation to this. Possibly the suffering is a ritual which purges Rambo and, more significantly, his empathizing viewers of guilt for failure in Vietnam. In order to be right, he has to be visibly and massively wronged. By extension, American audiences are granted an opportunity to see American involvement in the Vietnam War as righteous, the defeat to have been imposed on the military by amoral cowards above them.

Rambo is at war with himself, too. Some of the pain seems to be inflicted on himself. The star, Stallone, reportedly suggested that he hankers for pain, even at the level of fulfilling 'punishing' workouts to push his body to extremes. The curious result of the hard work that goes into the creation of the spectacular body is that it must be displayed. Display in the 1980s still seems strongly associated culturally with femininity or feminization. Therefore, the hypermasculinity suggested at an obvious level by

Figure 4.1   Rambo

Rambo's developed, armour-like body also suggests by its repeated display that it is given 'feminine' exposure to the spectator's gaze. The climactic violence of *First Blood* can be seen as an alibi for the body display.

The femininity associated with this display, and the masochistic suffering that Rambo so graphically undergoes, could drive a wedge between the spectator and the hero. Maybe scenes of masochism invite a sadistic, and thus emotionally distanced, response from the masculine spectator. Or perhaps, in taking this line, we have been seduced into believing what the official version of masculinity would have it as true – that masochism is a feminine pleasure confined to women. Perhaps the audience instead identifies strongly with Rambo in his more 'feminine' moments of victimization and body expos-ure. Perhaps masculinity is not as ignorant of the feminine as it purports to be.

WESTERNS

The western may be the supreme genre for the depiction of traditional, laconic, dominating masculinity. It combines the themes of the cowboy and his relationship with the frontier, of male potency and – till the later movies of John Wayne and Clint Eastwood – youth, of skill at gunplay. Moreover, while nearly all Hollywood narratives include a romance which culminates in marriage, cowboys can be such loners that at the end of the film they may ride into the sunset still alone. Thus, they evade domestication. Yet, they are portrayed as heterosexual, the protectors of women and also of men who are less efficient in the use of violence. Cowboy heterosexuality allows, though, for homosociality – the hero is often accompanied by a male sidekick or works with groups made up exclusively of men, such as posses.

If heterosexuality is the alibi for the cowboys' homosocial habits, the frontier alibis male violence. The need to tame the wild frontier has been made heroic by the rewriting of American history so that the 'injuns' become dangerous, cruel savages. Then, the model of the frontiersman animates (in an age when the frontier was closed) a nostalgia for a time and a male exemplar that valued male dominance. In times when men feel that masculinity has been diminished and that there are question marks over their value to the social organization, they can enjoy in fantasy a return to social conditions where strong, independent masculinity had unquestionable relevance.

A variant of the western, the sort of vigilante movie most famously epitomized in the 1970s by *Dirty Harry*, sometimes suggests, on the other hand, that society has become too soft, particularly in its compassion towards the criminal. Individual violence is used in this movie to protect Western civilization.

The western provides a world where men experience ageing without losing their power and authority. Chris Holmlund points out that such stars as Gary Cooper and James Stewart enjoy hero status in westerns made when the men themselves were far from youthful. She connects westerns' promotion of the idea that men, as they age, remain authoritative with a fantasy which is not confined to men and masculinity. Her observation is that with advancing years everybody denies age. She explains in part why hegemonic masculinity is so: 'we all participate in the same fears and fantasies' (Holmlund, 2002, p. 155).

WAR FILMS

One of the most influential studies of what was categorized by the author as 'soldier males' or 'soldier egos' is Klaus Theweleit's analysis of writings by the Freikorps. The Freikorps was a private army made up of volunteers who saw it as their mission to fight the revolutionary German working class after World War I. Theweleit sees such soldierly egos as the result of a failure to complete the process of separation from fusion with the mother in order to take a proper place in the world by becoming an individual. Their incompleteness is interpreted by him as the reason why soldier males of this sort feel combative towards all objects. These adult males are still trapped in the birth canal (Theweleit, 1985). As James Conlon puts it, 'The soft-fluid bodies of women ... [represent] both an enticing call to the womb-like bliss of the past and, by the same token, ... a harrowing attack on a fragile self-identity' (1990, p. 2). This double movement of repulsion and attraction is taken by Conlon to be illustrated by the distance from the woman experienced in the act of killing her, simultaneous with the closeness felt in penetrating her body in that act. The soldierly ego's obsession with machinery may be viewed as a response to the perceived need to clothe itself in armour against weakening sufficiently to surrender to the ever-present trap of emotions.

'Make love, not war' was a popular slogan of the 1960s which neatly separated the two activities. The sort of analysis undertaken by Theweleit suggests, however, that sex and battle may be confused in the psyche of the soldier male.

In 1987, Stanley Kubrick's *Full Metal Jacket* underlines the similarity between the initiation rites signifying that a boy has become a man, and basic training provided by the armed forces. In both, the male is removed from home and deprived of female company; his physical appearance is altered, in the GIs' case by the wearing of uniform and a close-cropped haircut. The kind of man that the boy has to become in the military is one who will concentrate on violent action to divert himself from the emotions summoned up by, say, the death of a friend.

There is a wider application, beyond the military context, to conceptions of masculinity in general. Military service, that most homosocial of worlds (second only, perhaps, to single-sex jails), emphatically denies and disavows its potential for homosexuality. Fear of homosexuality could help to explain masculinity's fear of intimacy in general, and why it easily tips over into misogyny and hatred of gay people.

Tony Scott's *Top Gun* (1986) illustrates the soldierly ego's fondness for combat, and for machinery with which to integrate instead of with the human self. Some of the most elating sequences of the movie are when Maverick (Tom Cruise) looks as if he has become one with his steel flying machine and soars in triumph over 'nature', represented by the sea and the sky. Male combat and male courting seem like parts of a similar process. The scene which serves as a link between Maverick's military and sexual successes is that in the classroom where Maverick stands up to a female instructor – resulting, it would seem, in the sequence in her home where she lies down for him. Later, when he loses confidence as a lover, this is restored by proof of his superiority in combat.

Hal Ashby's *Coming Home* (1978) shows men going off to Vietnam with their soldierly ego to the fore, but then returning to ask questions of this. Luke (Jon Voight) endures a physical paralysis which undermines his belief in the 'phallic' armour in which he had once dressed himself for battle. At first, he tries to hold on to his belief, provoking Sally (Jane Fonda), the woman with whom he falls in love, to ask, 'Why do you have to be such a bastard?'. Sally's husband, Bob (Bruce Dern), went off to war and now returns from it with the same defensive distance between himself and his wife. Unlike Bob, Luke abandons the masculinity that fears being swamped by female care of his person. It is as if his abandonment of the soldierly ego allows him to enjoy sexual intimacy. Sex is no longer a form of war. By contrast, Bob runs naked to his death, embracing the soldier male's most fundamental fear of dissolution of the self in the maternal 'feminine', symbolized by the sea.

The theme of post-Vietnam reassessment of the soldier male, and thus of a particular conception of masculinity, is returned to in several major movies, most notably in Michael Cimino's *The Deer Hunter* (1978) and Oliver Stone's *Born on the Fourth of July* (1989). Decades before these movies, the basic theme of the need for a new concept of masculinity is already the central concern of Fred Zinnemann's *The Men* (1950), made not many years after the end of World War II. Marlon Brando, in his first Hollywood starring role, plays the paraplegic hero forced to discard wartime belief in his physical superiority so that he may marry and accept loving, nurturing care from the Teresa Wright character. The relevance of this sort of psychological change to notions of masculinity is indicated with remarkable economy by the choice of title for this movie.

SLASHER MOVIES

The so-called slasher represents a sub-genre of horror. Moves to prohibit or confine the exhibition of slashers are made in the belief that repeated exposure to them will produce predictable antisocial effects. The basis for this belief is not as surely grounded in good evidence as it takes itself to be. Content analysis would suggest, in relation to, say, sexual violence to women, that there is little difference in the quantity of male and female deaths, while more female victims than male survive slashings. (There is, though, a possible difference in the 'quality' of the deaths, female victims' being more memorable because more salient.) Gloria Cowan and Margaret O'Brien go so far as to suggest that the message of slashers seems to be that masculinity needs to shed its excesses if males are to survive: 'Unmitigated masculinity ends in death, a historically modern message' (Cowan and O'Brien, 1990, p. 195). They note, among other factors, that male non-survivors tend to be cynical, foul-mouthed, self-centred and far more dictatorial than female non-survivors.

On the other hand, they interpret the portrayal of female non-survivors in essentially sexual terms as an indication that men enjoy graphic depictions of violence in horror more than women do.

Carol J. Clover is particularly interested in the survival of what she terms the 'final girl' at the end of slasher movies. If the audience is largely male, what appeal, she wonders, does the non-survival of the male victims but the survival of the victim-heroine have to it? Her conclusion in relation to gender is, 'What filmmakers seem to know better than film critics is that gender is less a wall than a permeable membrane' (Carol J. Clover, in Dines and Humez (eds), 1995, p. 179). Usually, the killer's masculinity is significantly compromised by his being, for example, transvestite or transsexual. Equally commonly, the 'final girl's' femininity is compromised by her wielding of the investigating gaze; it is also noteworthy that survival is more likely for women if they abstain from sexual behaviour. Thus, both these opposing characters combine masculinity and femininity.

Clover concludes that the 'final girl' is really a homoerotic stand-in: 'The discourse is wholly masculine, and females figure in it only insofar as they "read" some aspect of male experience' (Carol J. Clover, ibid., p. 181). Again, within the slasher movie, the woman's entire body is transformed by the male psychopathic killer into the 'bleeding wound' that signifies castration. Clearly, slashers concern male anxieties above all.

SPORTS MOVIES

The growing popularity of sports movies in the 1980s, and their often nostalgic nature, have been taken by Marjorie D. Kibby as a response to the recession of physical machismo as a lifestyle in the face of social and economic changes of the 1970s. Nostalgic sports movies, she believes, allowed black, homosexual and other marginalized masculinities to be temporarily elided and a highly stylized version of traditional masculinity to be reasserted (Kibby, 1998, p. 1).

In the 1970s, women and ethnic minorities were brought into the workplace. The speed of technological change suddenly devalued traditional male skills. Sport as represented in the movies reacquires, at this juncture, a particular relevance to masculinity: it offers a venue in which aggression, strength, competitiveness are valued and harnessed to the notion of that kind of masculinity as 'natural'.

To take but one example, *Field of Dreams*, the movie is not simply about baseball. It involves a return to an ideal of fatherhood. In that sense, it re-enacts the spiritual journey on which Robert Bly's *Iron John* sends men. The currently devalued father of this book must be reclaimed, together with his caring, life-giving power if men are to regain their potential. Ray Kinsella (Kevin Costner) needs to reconcile himself through baseball with the father he rebelled against in the 1960s if he is to rediscover the father within himself. As a corrective to Kibby's notion about the elision of black masculinity in these movies, the end of *Field of Dreams* at least has Terrence Mann ascending into heaven, to take his place among the bygone heroes of a sport which historically denied its black players. At the end of the movie, Ray plays outside with his dead father, while his wife remains a supremely domesticated homemaker. A myriad of baseball fans make their way to Ray's field in Iowa to behold the restored game and revivified, revered masculinity. This leads Bill Maurer to conclude that the American dream of nation and baseball is firmly rooted in gender (1992, p. 146).

'NEW BAD FUTURE' MOVIES

The term 'new bad future' and its definition as a future in which the world is in the grip of feverish decay are owed to Fred Glass. Glass links the NBF movie to society when he describes it as an unconscious vehicle to deal with the issues raised by the transition under capitalism, from a relatively stable mechanical/industrial society, to a less certain order where information technology replaces the national with the international (Glass, 1990, p. 3).

Far more human than either women or men in these movies are the cyborgs. Interest in the relation between body and machine has already been considered above, in light of Rambo's successful fusion of the technological and the 'natural'. Greater anxiety appears to be felt elsewhere about the future of masculinity in a technologically advanced environment. The space between the human and the technological may be seen as one of contestation.

Cyborgs are traditionally gendered. Arnold Schwarzenegger's Terminators are insistently male. Kibby takes the super-macho figure of the cyborg as a violent denial 'that there has been a feminization of technology, a change in the nature of work, and a greater acceptance of human sexual diversity' (1996, pp. 5–6). The cyborg movie is difficult to pin down to just one dominating interpretation. While women are sometimes written off in them as one-dimensional, fearful, anxious objects, they can be unusually 'strong'. The heroine of *Terminator II: Judgment Day* is recognizably in the mould of Sigourney Weaver's Ripley in the *Alien* series.

Schwarzenegger in *Total Recall* is, as in his cyborg roles, rendered unhuman by his muscle armour plating. The hero of this latter movie is symbolically castrated by virtue of his missing memory. His violence is necessitated by the need to get it back and regain control over his life. Glass suggests that one application of this is to our society as made up of amnesiacs: amnesia allows the rulers and the ruled to remain in their places (Glass, 1990, p. 7).

'MALE PARANOIA' MOVIES

Relatively recent US history may be read to suggest that normative gender roles were widely felt to be in crisis in the early 1970s, tottering under blows from feminism and gay and lesbian liberation, profoundly affected by experience of the war in Vietnam. The economic recession of the mid-1970s produced a backlash against activities by political minorities and anxiety about the loss of the war as a sign of decline in American imperial power. At its simplest, there was a new conception of the 'average US male' as victim – of such forces as feminism, gay liberation, affirmative action, the onward march of history.

Men in such 1980s movies as *The Right Stuff* are seen as loners, confronting the feminine within themselves in order to conquer it. They are also, as portrayed in, say, the *Rambo* movies (see above) and *Lethal Weapon*, objects of the gaze. There is consciousness of femininity, both in terms of their psychology and their playing to a male gaze. There is also, though, vigorous combating of that through aggressive hypermasculinity or, as we have seen in the section on spectatorship in Chapter 3, through disavowal. If violence is unusually inner-directed in Rambo's masochist mode, it is directed, with lethal efficiency, outwards too.

The slasher sub-genre specializes in women-in-peril. A similar, but counter, theme is explored in relation to men in the 1980s and 1990s. *Fatal Attraction, Basic Instinct* and *Falling Down* all centre on a man-in-peril. All star the same man, Michael Douglas, who at this point makes a career out of playing the male as victim. The particular inflection of this victim hero in *Falling Down* is constantly assailed and degraded by an impressive variety of tormentors – his wife, chicano gangs, shopkeepers, over-meticulous managers of fast-food restaurants. The violence which he perpetrates as a sign that he is standing up to his persecutors, rather than falling down before them, was reportedly applauded by males in the audience. The 'average white US male' has only violence to turn to, it would seem, to restore his sense of masculinity when it is threatened by social change, unemployment, the plurality of American social organization.

These male-victim movies share with Quentin Tarantino's *Reservoir Dogs* the likely explanation that they are a form of 'return of the repressed'. What was repressed in the 1970s, the period of Tarantino's childhood, returns in physically violent, monstrous form in the 1990s, and arguably earlier in 1980s' male paranoia movies. Amy Taubin thinks of *Reservoir Dogs* as 'such a 1990s film' because 'it's about the repression of 1970s masculinity – a paranoid, homophobic fear of the other that explodes in hate speech, in kicks and blows, in bullets and blades' (Amy Taubin, quoted in Smith (ed.), 1996, p. 128).

COMEDY

Comedies tend to illuminate a different side to, or different version of, masculinity. The comedic hero is vulnerable. If he is depicted as self-controlled, stoical, imperturbable, it is almost certainly in order to satirize the traditional notion of masculinity.

Nicole Matthews notices that, in more recent comedies, fatherhood is more likely to be presented as a problem than motherhood. The particular kind of fatherhood that is approved in such movies as *Back to the Future* is a version where fathers behave in a way that is remarkably similar to the behaviour of their sons. The fundamental requirement of approved fatherhood is that the father is physically present and, in that particular but limited sense, supportive. Comedies of fatherhood spend very little time confronting the details of parental responsibility. Parenting is 'emptied of content', in Matthews' words (2000, p. 116).

The temptation to read the depiction of fathers in film comedy as a direct comment on men, or more narrowly on fathers, should be resisted, however. The separation in some comedies of fatherliness from biological fatherhood, and the equation of fatherly behaviour with filial behaviour, suggest that the message of such movies could be restricted to promotion of the norm of responsibility. The norm seems to be related to parenting in general, intended as much for women as for men, but also to nurturing and caring beyond the family, in family-like situations. Matthews instances the gay and lesbian community's care for homosexual AIDS patients to show how widely the lesson of responsibility may be disseminated (ibid., p. 133).

ILLNESS MOVIES

Movies' consideration of AIDS shows such unwillingness to face this major health crisis as to be largely silent about the subject. Discussions of movies' representation of AIDS, my own book-length discussion included (MacKinnon, 1992), are forced to examine the probability that any addressing of the pandemic is highly oblique, almost never direct.

While it is difficult not to see the relevance of AIDS to such 1980s' movies as *Fatal Attraction* and *The Fly*, most movies that address the subject of lethal illness in a post-AIDS world do so in the context of heterosexual males. As Robert Eberwein puts it, talking of such heroes, 'Their capacity to heal seems to be bound up in a complex way with their masculinity and heterosexuality, which are affirmed even from the grave' (1995, p. 155).

The hero of *Born on the Fourth of July* is incapacitated by his paraplegia, but does not die. In the course of the film, the resurgence of (a different form of) masculinity and heterosexuality is celebrated. Male characters presented with problems of paralysis or terminal cancer in recent movies struggle, notably with the help of women as sexual healers, back to fuller sexual potential.

In contrast, characters with AIDS have to leave off their sexual activity. *The Living End* may seem an exception to this, but here sexual indulgence is intimately linked with the embrace of death as the characters' destiny. Even when AIDS is totally absent from some movies, it may be highly interesting that a homosexual character is depicted as peculiarly vulnerable to physical illness from which he cannot hope to recover. 'Straight' men will improve, even if not fully restored to health. Even in a relatively upbeat comedy such as Mike Newell's *Four Weddings and a Funeral*, the funeral is reserved for the homosexual character played by Simon Callow.

PORNOGRAPHY

A quite different example of the attention paid to the difference between heterosexual and homosexual delineation may be found in the field of erotica. The male presented as an erotic object for heterosexual women seems largely to be the reasonably attractive but distinctly average man. Males offered as erotic objects for homosexual men are idealized, rendered unusually handsome, virile, dominating and phallic. This is reminiscent of the way that women are idealized, this time to be beautiful, ultra-feminine, submissive to the male sexual will, for the apparent benefit of heterosexual males. It is thus easy to reach the obvious conclusion that erotic images aimed at the male demand an idealized representation of sexual attractiveness in physical terms.

One of the most evident myths in heterosexual pornography is that men are perpetually ready to perform sexually, just as women are perpetually available and eager for that performance. This sort of mythology leads Harry Brod to conclude that sex is mechanized, the pleasure of sex reduced, by the sort of self-consciousness that distances the male from intimacy with his female lover. Against the view that pornography expresses not male powerfulness but the male's social experience of powerlessness, Brod prefers the explanation that pornography acts in two different directions: it expresses men's public power; it also expresses men's lack of 'authentic personal power'. He sums this up by suggesting that it expresses the power of alienated sexuality, or perhaps the alienated power of sexuality (Harry Brod, in Hearn and Morgan (eds), 1990, p. 134). Something which is widely believed to teach the domination of women ends up as something which dominates men themselves.

INDIVIDUAL MOVIES

A few movies are discussed individually below, before two individual stars are similarly discussed, because work relevant to the representation of masculinity has been published on them.

BORN ON THE FOURTH OF JULY

Don Kunz's article on Oliver Stone's 1989 film considers it in relation to the book of the same title (Kunz, 1990). He believes that the film should be taken as an exception to the notion that the bulk of Vietnam War considerations in literature and film favour a return to traditional gender roles which serve the interests of patriarchy. According to Kunz, the heroic masculine ideal enshrined in frontier history is re-examined and found wanting (ibid., pp. 23–24).

Instead of positively promoting patriarchal domination over 'feminized' others, Stone's film exposes the catastrophic results of such domination. The American frontier myth (shown above to be vital to the construction of masculinity within westerns and vigilante movies in particular) is exploited to give the US licence to perpetrate violence abroad. The father of Ron Kovic's (Tom Cruise) family is rejected in favour of heroic archetypes. Young men before their enlistment define themselves in relation to America's mythic past (ibid., p. 6).

The movie shows the damage done to individuals by 'masculine' attitudes based on an amalgam of patriotism, religion and an emphasis on the importance of winning, with its demand for physical strength.

The pre-Vietnam portion indicates the binary oppositions on which traditional masculinity seems to rest: to win, others must be losers; to live, others must die; to be a man, others must be women or feminized. It is feminizing to feel compassion or to fail (in high-school wrestling, here) (ibid., pp. 6–7).

Interestingly for the present study, movies and television – as well as Roman Catholicism, high school and sport – are indicted in the book (and film of the book) for teaching the receptive young Kovic small-town values, such as those of hard work, competition, duty and sacrifice. In his book, Kovic singles out the John Wayne war movie *The Sands of Iwo Jima* and Audie Murphy's star vehicle *To Hell and Back* for updating American frontier myth so that the archetypal American male is envisaged as establishing civilization amid savagery. This image sends Kovic to Vietnam. It is shockingly turned round over there, so that the savagery seems to be that of the American military (ibid., pp. 1–2).

DEAD RINGERS

David Cronenberg's *Dead Ringers* is discussed by Barbara Creed in terms of its alleged 'phallic panic', which she understands in relation to male hysteria (Creed, 1990).

Freud, acknowledging that hysteria is not confined to women as was commonly believed before him, permits it to be thought of in the case of males as a defence against the possibility of symbolic castration. Hysteria was explained by Freud as a psychological reaction in men who failed to take up what he thought of as the proper masculine role. Like women, men may express their distress and conflicts through hysterical bodily symptoms: the result of seeing female genitals, a sight which provokes castration anxiety in men according to Freud, might be manifested as vision impairment, for instance (ibid., pp. 129–133).

Creed interprets the Cronenberg movie, with its male twin doctors and a woman with an 'impossible' forked womb – it forks into three, the movie asks us to believe – as a prime example of the representation of male hysteria. 'The signs of phallic panic which run through *Dead Ringers* point to the impossible nature of the narcissistic fantasy which lies at the heart ... of masculinity' (ibid., p. 146).

THE CRYING GAME

Neil Jordan's celebrated film of 1993 is discussed by J. Boozer, Jr as a demonstration of how the social invades the personal. It does not treat the personal as somehow an alternative to the political (Boozer, 1995, p. 174). The hold of phallocentrism – an insistence on the phallic logic of patriarchy – is loosened, as the old certainties of sex and politics are shaken. The audience's sudden change of perception of Dil's (Jaye Davidson) sexual identity epitomizes this loosening. Moreover, as the narrative advances, so the hero Fergus (Stephen Rea) is increasingly feminized. In London, where he is 'Jimmy' rather than Fergus, his main personal concern is Dil. Boozer draws a wider message from Fergus's relationship with Dil: 'his experience with Dil not only demonstrates how the political and sexual remain intertwined, but how constricted definitions of masculine and feminine heterosexuality support patriarchal hegemony' (ibid.).

Patriarchy requires femininity to be weaker, to need masculine support, to give masculinity its meaning. Dil is not in any straightforward sense a woman, and yet she is clearly, to an extent, rendered feminine when the audience is misled as to the character's gender. Fergus does not experience sexual fulfilment with Dil and is shown not to be Dil's master, however protective his instincts towards her. The emotional need could be shown to be his (ibid., p. 175).

The one biologically female character in *The Crying Game* is Jude (Miranda Richardson). She comes off badly, in ethical terms, in comparison with Dil. She demands a clear separation of the personal and the political. For her, Irish nationalism must be given priority over not only sexual orientation, but humanity itself. She is identified by Boozer as a phallic woman (ibid., p. 173) in her religious devotion to a political ideology. While she uses her sex to capture the British soldier Jody (Forrest Whitaker), this is not the equivalent of a *femme fatale*'s castrating seduction in film noir. Her convictions are those of IRA dogma.

The positive characters abandon phallocentrism, in Boozer's view. Both Dil and Fergus finally choose to follow paths that depart from those of dominant notions of heterosexuality and race. Phallocentrism is political in this movie – it is fascistic, according to Boozer. The essay concludes, 'Positive male characters are forced into more flexible, emotionally supportive roles, whereas positive feminine characters are pressed into becoming more assertive' (ibid., p. 176).

THE FULL MONTY

Rosalind Coward (1999) considers *The Full Monty* in the course of her book, *Sacred Cows: Is Feminism Relevant to the New Millennium?* She recognizes that it taps into a highly contemporary concern with men's roles, particularly in the context of large-scale male redundancy. By the end of the film, with the men embarked on a new career as strippers for female audiences, they have learned that their one asset is their ability to sell their bodies. This, ironically, was long thought to apply only to women because of their economic powerlessness. A major concern of society seems, on evidence such as this, to be a kind of gender revolution, where ignorant sexism is replaced by the question of how men must live in a new world of independent women (Coward, 1999, p. 62).

She contrasts this film with *Brassed Off*, which she sees as a very 1980s' film, with a now old-fashioned left-wing agenda: male prejudice and management's inhumanity to its workers (ibid., p. 61).

As a possible curb to over-estimation of *The Full Monty*'s daring or modernity, Justine Wyatt notes how traditional its view of homosexuality is, and particularly how clear and unbridgeable is the division between it and heterosexuality (Justine Wyatt, in Lehman (ed.), 2001, p. 62).

RANSOM

The subtitle to Krin Gabbard's essay on this 1996 movie clarifies that *Ransom* is to be discussed as an example of 'resurgent white masculinity' (Krin Gabbard, in Lehman (ed.), 2001). The hero, Tom Mullen (Mel Gibson), is a family man but spends much of the movie asserting his manhood in violation of family conventions (ibid., p. 9). He is thus an incoherent representation of both family man and cinematic man of action.

Mainstream Hollywood cinema usually suggests that masculine autonomy is retained through the hero's resistance to marriage. (This is illustrated with particular clarity by the classic western ending of the hero riding off alone into the sunset.) Mullen, however, contrives to be the man of action from within the setting of the family. When the myth of the American hero meets those of the bourgeois family, Gabbard states, something's got to give (ibid., p. 10). The particular example of this from within the movie is that the hero defies wife and agent and takes an entirely individual decision to refuse the ransom. The family is reunited and the hero vindicated at the end.

The American hero is traditionally conceived of as masculine. Heroic masculinity is careful not to allow itself to be watered down, or feminized. This is what devotion to the family ideal threatens to do. Here, the threat is avoided by a keypoint refusal of the family's demands – though not to the ultimate detriment of that family.

The 1993 *Falling Down* (touched on above) is usually cited by critics as exemplifying the challenge to maleness from blacks, women, and groups that were previously disempowered. There, though, a divided reading is invited for the hero's violent reactions to that challenge. The audience may not be united in its evaluation of them and him. The audience for *Ransom*, however, is expected to identify fully with Mullen. His fight against feminizing others – his wife, the (black) agent – is never allowed to be seen as the result of male paranoia. Gabbard concludes that Tom Mullen has more in common with Forrest Gump than D-Fens, the Michael Douglas character of *Falling Down* (ibid., p. 19).

MALE STARS

Stardom is vitally connected with questions of gender. Put most simply, certain stars are known to have had particular appeal for women, others for men. Joan Mellen, for example, names silent-screen star Rudolph Valentino and Robert Redford as having special appeal to women, John Wayne and Clint Eastwood to men, while, she believes, stars such as Clark Gable and Humphrey Bogart were the stuff of fantasy for both men and women (Mellen, 1978, p. 4).

This relatively clear division is more blurred today. In more recent times, Schwarzenegger, for example, is less easy to interpret in this straightforward fashion. He may be thought of more as a postmodern icon. His laconicism and repression of the emotional are part of a tradition of hypermasculinity, a tradition where Clint Eastwood and Charles Bronson have their place. Yet, he is also a figure of parody for the same reasons. In other words, he seems to demand to be interpreted partly through the use of irony. He is not to be 'taken straight'.

WARREN BEATTY

Dennis Bingham notes, with regard to Warren Beatty as star figure, how he both confirms and undermines certain key tenets of Laura Mulvey's influential account (discussed under 'Gendered spectatorship' in Chapter 3). That is, he may not be reducible to an object of the female gaze yet, at the same time, female characters in his films are usually the subjects. In this way, Beatty's version of masculinity is multiple and contradictory. He is both exhibitionist and self-effacing. In his case, 'objectification [is] so subtle it can be mistaken for its opposite' (Bingham, 1994, p. 154).

In *McCabe and Mrs Miller* and his own production, *Shampoo*, Beatty not only shows his feminine side, but is also is manifestly close to women, even if his characters are called on to deny that closeness. In *Bonnie and Clyde*, his character is sexually impotent. Bonnie is better at robbing banks and is a more rounded person.

Bingham concludes that Beatty is a muddle in gender terms, and that his masculinity is unsettling to male spectators. He is 'too distant, too contradictory and incoherent, and perhaps friendly with all those women in ways that imply the inferiority of other men' (ibid., p. 162).

CLINT EASTWOOD

Dennis Bingham again, this time on Eastwood, notes how the private persona of the star is difficult to bring into an account of his particular stardom. Since Richard Dyer's seminal book on stars (Dyer, 1998), it has been customary to see the carefully managed 'image' of a star as private person as a vital part of the overall star image. This image, of the extra-cinematic person, feeds back into the cinema image. Conversely, the image of the star gained from his/her performances on screen feeds back into the image of the extra-cinematic person. In Eastwood's case, though, his wife and children were seldom photographed. Yet, his apparent dependence on family life runs against the fiercely independent characters of Dirty Harry or the hero of the spaghetti westerns, The Man With No Name. When he is publicized in 'real-person' terms, it tends to be as mayor of the town of Carmel (Bingham, 1990, pp. 33–34).

Intriguingly, Bingham discerns a particular value in the incompleteness and shadowy quality of the star. Eastwood is, by this explanation, the outline whose desires and motivations the spectator fills in on his behalf. His minimalism means that he is like a blank paper on which spectators can write their own preoccupations (ibid., p. 43).

Paul Smith is interested in the way that Eastwood is often presented in terms of a masochistic object, not only suffering pain and humiliation, but constituting an object of the gaze – his naked walk nearly the length of the penitentiary close to the beginning of *Escape from Alcatraz* is the clearest example of the latter. Smith, though, notes the signs of disavowal when an Eastwood character is objectified, and the fact that any overpowering or degradation of his character is always *temporary*, a stage in the narrative where the male body is tested (Paul Smith, in Berger, Wallis, Watson (eds), 1995, pp. 85, 87).

If the look at Eastwood's characters is in some senses deflected through disavowal, it is not the look that Laura Mulvey argues is traditional for the male subject of

Hollywood movies. She believes that the spectator's look is mapped on to the male protagonist's look, that we look through his eyes. But how would that work with Eastwood? After all, in Bingham's view, he does not look, because he does not need to see in order to know for sure. Eastwood's look is impenetrable and thus unreadable. The spectator is responsible for the looking in Eastwood movies. In that sense, it is the spectator's desire that animates the film (Bingham, 1990, p. 45).

In an even more complex argument about Eastwood in *Tightrope*, Ron Burnett thinks of his character's desires as the opposite of what that character is taken to represent. He is a single parent with two beautiful daughters, as well as the detective who hunts down killers of women. The relationship between who he seems to be and what he desires is tortured and confusing. This could be an explanation for his voice in this movie as uncertain, weak and sometimes silent (Burnett, 1985, p. 77).

Burnett argues that Eastwood's character's sexuality is a form of bondage. This aspect of the movie is taken to comment on the fantasies of other films, especially those of pornography (discussed above in terms of sexual alienation). He does not see himself as the killer of women to whom he makes love, but attributes the enactment of his desires to the intrusion of an 'other'.

Both Bingham and Burnett are aware of 'absence' as an important element in this star's maintenance of masculine characterization. By Eastwood's distancing himself from them, his characters manage not to be responsible for their psychological drives. The audience is confronted with its own desires, and to that extent with its role in animating the narrative. Or else the character divides into a conscious part and refuses responsibility for the unconscious, which is projected on to an 'other' outside the hero's cognition.

These analyses of Eastwood as star inevitably also suggest that the maintenance of masculinity may involve massive denial and even self-delusion.

HARD BODIES/SOFT BODIES

Susan Jeffords believes that the masculine body is central to popular culture and national identity. It is to her that we owe the idea that this body – in the sense of body image – changed between the Reagan and Bush presidencies, and that there had already been a change in those years from what obtained in the years of President Carter. The so-called soft body is associated with the latter period. The hard body, on the other hand, is an image which was expected during Reagan's presidencies to counteract the soft-body image of the Carter years. In the 1980s, the hard body suited a foreign policy that was stoutly militaristic. Yet, according to Jeffords, this was also the period of the 'sensitive family man', when family values were lauded, with the father being the linchpin of the domestic set-up. She argues that the conception of the hard body alters again in the later 1980s and early 1990s, when it is re-evaluated.

From this point, masculine strength is associated with internal, personal values demonstrated through men's relations with their families (Jeffords, 1994, p. 13).

Popular culture does not, of course, neatly and schematically back up the change from soft- to hard-body image simply in the transition from the Carter presidency to that of Reagan. There were, Jeffords concedes, hard-body movies in the 1970s: the Clint Eastwood vehicles, *Dirty Harry* and *Magnum Force*, for example, or the vigilante films such as 1974's *Death Wish*.

Nevertheless, these hard-body movies of the 1970s may be distinguished from the sort that prevailed in the Reagan years. Dirty Harry and his ilk took their lone stands in defiance of their societies. The heroes of 1980s' hard-body movies defied government bureaucracies and institutions that were self-serving enough to have lost touch with society. Their defiance becomes, in this way, an act of solidarity with the citizens of their society, and a 'wake-up call', to use a current cliché.

An allied view of the same changes in movie heroes, but argued towards a different conclusion, is offered by Marj Kibby (1996). She recognizes that masculinity becomes increasingly unsure of itself in the 1970s. The technologizing of the workplace was increasingly and speedily developed, new groups introduced to the workforce, old established industries replaced by new. All of this meant that men could no longer be sure of where they stood in the economic system, and that male identity itself had been destabilized. For Kibby, 'The hegemonic masculinity represented in the cinema of the eighties was not so much perceived masculine identity, but more an hysterical response to an apparent lack of identity' (ibid., p. 3).

The combination of hard-bodied and sensitive, family-oriented characteristics is already apparent in the close father–son bonding of *Star Wars* in 1977, but is given renewed force by 1989's *Indiana Jones and the Last Crusade*, for example. All three *Back to the Future* movies explore the theme of the past's continuity with the present through the father–son relationship. The father–son dynamic replaces and eliminates others. Thus, in Vietnam films, according to Jeffords, feminism, communism, revolution, like women, Vietnamese and blacks, are denied and defeated (1988, p. 487). The effect is to suggest that American wars are fought by and for the male family bond of fathers and sons. The father's position must be restabilized for there to be an end to violence.

The serious and proper concern of masculinity with family is already heavily signalled in the 1970s, with *The Godfather*. Don Corleone's three sons weaken patriarchy by dividing male authority among three different lifestyles. A single strong authority, a father, is the answer. Family must be recreated in the patriarchal mould – that is, under a strong patriarch. This prefigures the energy expended under Reagan and Bush in the bid to restore the father and thus patriarchy.

The reduction of complex issues to a simple, single explanation accords well with the anti-politics bias of Reagan's presidency. What is opposed is the idea that a worthwhile aim can be achieved by collective political struggle. Politics is made to seem bogus and corrupt, government itself self-serving.

1991 is taken to be a year of special significance by Susan Jeffords. It is at that point that she detects the clearest evidence in movies that the heroic Americans represented by Arnold Schwarzenegger, Bruce Willis and Chuck Norris give way to a different sort of hero – and thus, that their particular hard bodies alter for another version of the hard body. Schwarzenegger himself changes drastically from being the emotionless killing machine of the original *Terminator* (1984) to the family man (or robot!) of *Terminator 2: Judgment Day* in 1991.

This change, among several, most economically illustrates the basic point, that a new sort of hero is required, still hard-bodied and able to fight, but only in order to protect – a hero who has feelings and acts on them. Fred Pfeil, on the evidence of *Regarding Henry*, *The Fisher King* and *Hook* dubs 1991 'the year of living sensitively' (Pfeil, 1995, p. 37). Through such movies, audiences are persuaded that professional managerial lifestyles are the norm in society. In the 1980s, male rampage is a dominant theme of movies. By 1991, the most popular seems to be the initial alienation of the hero and, through suffering, his reconnection to his family and thus to the world. These more sensitive heroes (re)discover the child in them. They must also hold on to paternal power, though, and find a way of accommodating their sense of joy in family, with authority over others in that family.

The hard body remains a white body. Danny Glover, playing the family man of *Lethal Weapon*, does not combine family commitment with taking a leading part in saving the nation or an important corporation. He has already shown the sensitivity required of the post-1990 hero, but not his sense of mission. The 'new' but still white hard-body hero of the 1990s does not take account of his racial and economic privileges.

This is but one important illustration of the general point, that larger social and political concerns are refused admission to cinematic considerations of masculinity in the 1990s. The promotion of the childlike hero, with heart in the right place but head nowhere to be seen, is most obvious of all in *Forrest Gump*. Through it – and the commercial success it enjoyed was huge – straight, white masculinity is represented in this new guise. The childlike but right-thinking Gump is unable to comprehend the complexity and near chaos of the politics through which he has lived. His decision to stay out of both politics and the complexity of society, and to concentrate instead on taking care of his own, seems to say a lot about notions of masculinity in this decade.

If we return to popular culture of the 1980s through the perspective of the 1990s, then we may 'read' 1980s' hard-body entertainment with a different emphasis from that available in the period. Violence was forced upon movie heroes. They merely responded, effectively, to outside forces. In choosing the path of duty and being so single-mindedly devoted to it, though, these men inadvertently denied themselves family, so that they seem in the next decade lonely and pained. In that sense, by doing their jobs too well, without a thought for themselves, they have been self-destructive.

1980s' hypermasculinity becomes a liability in the 1990s. Schwarzenegger becomes not just the good guy in the second *Terminator*, but takes the title role in *Kindergarten Cop* (1991, once again). He becomes more paternal than actual fathers. The latent paternalism in good guys of the 1990s is already suggested by the treatment of masculinity in *Three Men and a Baby* and *Look Who's Talking* in the late 1980s. Once again, the previous decade feeds into 1990s' conceptions of masculinity or suggests developments for the 1990s' through embryonic ideas from the 1980s.

The absence of contention with the social or political context, even at the level of ideas, may explain why 1991 films, for example, so often feature transformation and yet remain vague at the end about the futures of the transformed protagonists. External reasons are suggested for the heroes' impoverished life before the transformation, but there is no suggestion that they will do anything after it about the social structures which damaged them and their families. Concentration, instead, is on the self and how to improve it – in the spheres of health, family and home, but not beyond.

MASCULINITY AS A PROBLEM

The problem at the heart of movie masculinity today is exposed by the way that it is so insistent on its heterosexuality. Once, masculinity was defined in contrast to femininity, and so to women and to effeminate men. Today, it seems as if the once separate categories of women and homosexual men have entirely collapsed into one another. Perhaps because movies no longer dare to depict women as nurturing and domesticated, they do the next best thing, as it were, and make gay men nurturing and domesticated. 'Gay men have become today's women,' Amy Aronson and Michael Kimmel conclude (in Lehman (ed.), 2001, p. 47). In order to keep gay men in that role, they are made asexual, uninterested in having sex themselves but concerned with the love lives of heterosexual women in particular.

The men who are nurturing and caring are kept at a distance from masculinity. Nevertheless, machismo is no longer a safe role for men to take on. Men in post-Vietnam movies never quite regain unquestioning or unquestioned paternalist authority.

Curiously, it may be that questions raised about masculinity in the movies only apparently concern gender. There are several commentators who would alert us to the possibility that, through questions of that sort, quite other problems are addressed and explored. For example, questions of class may be raised by, say, *Someone to Watch Over Me*, where a (married) working-class man is attracted to an upper-class woman. Stanley Aronowitz suggests that in such instances being working class is identified with masculinity, being upper class with femininity. From this observation, he goes on to suggest that today's movies code sex, class and power interchangeably (Aronowitz, 1992, pp. 205, 208).

The opposite is, however, suggested by Peter Biskind and Barbara Ehrenreich. They believe that *Saturday Night Fever, Blue Collar, Rocky I* and *II* seem to be about the working class, but are actually about 'the man question' (Biskind and Ehrenreich, 1980, p. 110). This happens because by the late 1970s those male virtues that were no longer socially acceptable in the middle class – virtues such as physical endurance or deep loyalty among men – could be projected on to the working class. While class is, according to these writers, depoliticized, masculinity has been politicized. Defiant masculinity is the only source of subversion on the cinematic landscape. Its link with the working class is, though, highly nostalgic. Hollywood's working class, they believe, lives in a world whose time has gone by (ibid., p. 130).

If class is used to distinguish masculinities – machismo causing less question if associated with working-class representation – something similar could be said about ethnicity. The example already cited in this chapter of the black cop's easy, integrated relationship with his family and his white partner's estrangement from his, in *Lethal Weapon*, perhaps rings the changes. Black masculinity is often associated, especially in the 1970s, with machismo and traditional, dominant masculinity.

The above paragraphs suggest why it might be reasonable to speculate that, where masculinity is the theme, still other ideological and political conflicts are worked through under that heading.

Masculinity was created in classic Hollywood to keep the male superior, whatever the physical evidence to the contrary. Hollywood gave false teeth to Clark Gable and James Dean, made Alan Ladd stand on boxes to make him seem taller than his leading ladies; machismo was asserted even in male stars' monosyllabic names – for example, 'John Wayne' for Marion Michael Morrison. There is supposed to be nothing to stretch credulity in the way that visibly ageing stars, some with toupees, attract young women. Think of Audrey Hepburn yearning in the 1950s for Humphrey Bogart (*Sabrina Fair*), or Gary Cooper (*Love in the Afternoon*), or for Cary Grant in the 1960s (*Charade*). How different is this from the 1990s' sexual chemistry supposed to be sparked off between Sean Connery and Catherine Zeta Jones?

Joan Mellen's belief is that men cannot live by the masculinity on offer from Hollywood. There can be no illusions, she declares, on men's part about resembling the heroes of classic movies. The ease with which the evidence of age and decay are swept away and not allowed to form a barrier to women's fascination with these movie gods makes ordinary men feel less adequate, she would have it (Mellen, 1978, p. 5). Perhaps they should feel inadequate, if we follow workaday logic. All the same, cinema narrative weaves potent fantasies, including the fantasy of extreme potency.

The thinking of psychoanalyst Jacques Lacan traces all our 'misrecognitions' to the mirror phase where the infant, looking at its reflection, sees something more than itself, and believes in its own powers as greater than they are. The man looking at the movie screen commonsensically knows that he is not the hero – he is not as strong or handsome or, for that matter, as well lit, or so often photographed from a low angle or equipped with a convincing wig when his hair thins. In his strong sense of identification with him, common sense does not apply all that well, though.

THREE RECENT ILLUSTRATIONS

All popular movies offer some sort of message about masculinity. The following three, all from the year 2000, are especially interesting because of the way that they foreground questions of masculinity.

AMERICAN PSYCHO (MARY HARRON)

Patrick Bateman (Christian Bale), the 'psycho' of the title, is a serial killer who loses count of his killings. A tiresome male friend and a homeless man (and his dog) are despatched with brutal suddenness. However, his victims of choice are female. His victimization of women extends to his sexual and erotic relations with them.

Bateman's being a mass murderer is treated here as though this is a hideously extreme, but recognizable, extension of his spiritual emptiness, preening narcissism and selfish greed as a man – and as a Wall Street yuppie of 1987, practising the lifestyle lauded by Ronald Reagan in the US, by Margaret Thatcher in the UK. Although his male peers exchange mildly anxious glances when he holds forth with particular bile about women, their own leisure repartee is full of misogyny. So homophobic is he that, hilariously, one of his would-be victims escapes strangulation because he cannot bear to touch him, even while wearing gloves, which he washes compulsively when the victim misinterprets the placing of his hands on his neck.

Bateman seems to have almost no personal history. He has constructed himself out of glossy men's magazines, regarding himself as an expert in male fashion, grooming, restaurants, the music of Huey Lewis, Phil Collins and Whitney Houston. He is, as he confides to the soundtrack, not really there. He is all surface. When he hires women for sex, he camcords the action, and often regards his naked, much-exercised 'hard body' in the mirror with more fascination than his sex objects.

When finally his violence appears to be partly or wholly fantasized, and his secretary (Chloe Sevigny) is left sadly leafing through pages of sketches of tortured and brutalized women in his desk diary, Harron's point remains: that Bateman stands for the brand of masculinity just beneath the civilized surface of US, though especially Reaganite, society.

WHAT WOMEN WANT (NANCY MEYERS)

Advertising executive Nick Marshall (Mel Gibson) is jolted by electricity when a hair dryer falls into his bath in the course of his attempts to research what it feels like to be a woman. The accident suddenly gifts him with the ability to hear women's thoughts. At first, he uses this power to steal his female boss's ideas or to enjoy a one-night stand with a smitten admirer before dumping her. Yet, this being a romantic comedy, he learns ultimately to respect women's vulnerability.

The movie roots his objectification of women in his infancy as a showgirl's pampered child. Although his adult attitudes are those a beer-commercial man, his advertising firm needs to tap into the women's market, recognizing that females from 16 to 24 are the fastest-growing consumer group in the country.

The 'man's man' that the unreconstructed Nick represents is usefully defined by his ex-wife early in the movie as one that garners the admiration of other men, and that loves women's bodies but is confused and scared by their feelings.

What he first hears from women's minds is a babel of voices talking of calorie counts and make-up colours. Disconcertingly, he also hears a woman to whom he is making love wondering, 'Is Britney Spears on Leno tonight?'. Women in the office only pretend to like him. One loathes everything about him but his 'sweet little ass'.

Love changes his attitudes. Instead of feeling disgust at intimacy, he learns empathy. His wardrobe changes from black outfits, leather jackets, close-fitting shirts to blue, brown, white, and less aggressive styles.

Figure 4.2 What Women Want

What women want, the question whose answer eluded Sigmund Freud, is here answered: a man willing to listen to them when they express their concerns. Yet, these are concerns created by a male-oriented commercial culture. This insultingly simplistic answer is matched by another insult, that the movie's climax involves a Nike commercial for female runners, as if patriarchy alone can provide the solutions for the problems it has created.

BILLY ELLIOT (STEPHEN DALDRY)

This British movie made a sufficient impression in the US to be a contender for the 2001 Academy Awards.

Underlying the family conflict raging around Billy's (Jamie Bell) ambition to be a ballet dancer is the fear that ballet will make him less masculine. According to his working-class father, Jack (Gary Lewis), 'Lads do football, boxing, or wrestling – not friggin' ballet.' This loss of masculinity seems to be equated with homosexuality. A sign of the movie's sophistication is the way that ultimately neither Billy nor it rises to the bait. Billy and his pal Michael remain friends after the latter is discovered wearing a dress. He politely declines a little girl's offer to show him her 'fanny'. When he tells Michael, 'Just because I like ballet doesn't mean I'm a poof', that is an end to the debate. The film does not explore his sexuality further, because to do so would probably mean that the idea of its relevance to the notion of his masculinity would be

Figure 4.3 Billy Elliot

validated. Billy's goal is artistry, which he wastes no time on relating to questions of sexual 'normality'.

The boy is tender to his senile grandmother in a way that suggests he not only grieves for his dead mother, but becomes a version of her in the family home. Jack and his older brother, those who are most concerned about questions of masculinity, are striking miners caught up in the fight with Margaret Thatcher's government. Perhaps it is because they endure the 'feminization' of not working and not being breadwinners that Billy's love of dance angers them so.

If the movie surprises by refusing to enter into debates about sexuality, its principal surprise concerns Jack. He is cast almost as the villain of the piece, until his pride in his son's skills and the reawakening of a sense of parental responsibility persuade him to do the unthinkable, to cross the picket line, to become a 'scab', so that he can afford Billy's audition in London with the Royal Ballet School. The tenderness dammed up in him is released by Billy's confidence in his male identity and his determination to succeed. The bonding of father and son suggests that men as well as women, straight as well as gay, need to face up to hitherto unrecognized oppression.

Often glibly dismissed as a 'feel-good' fairy tale, *Billy Elliot* features a climactic departure from his family and home where the cathartic release of loving feelings coincides with the hero's being placed beyond and out of touch with them. The town returns to its customary routines, and to the sense of despair that the collapse of the miners' strike engenders. His success means inevitable loss to the adults surrounding him – but also, thus, to himself. If traditional masculinity is superseded, it is at the cost of separation from the bearers of tradition and the working-class family itself.

IN CONCLUSION

Certain ideas recur with remarkable regularity in the accounts of genres, movies, film stars and trends in male representation discussed above.

One particularly popular notion is that in social terms, men's confidence in their masculinity was shaken badly by changes in the 1970s. Not only was traditional masculinity severely critiqued by feminism, men's traditional skills in the workplace were sidelined by technological advances. These advances in turn meant that women were as well placed as men to undertake technologically sophisticated tasks. With one of the key elements in male self-confidence – their breadwinner status – destabilized, men had to ask questions of themselves, concerning the meaning of old-fashioned masculinity in a new world of mass unemployment and its relevance to, for example, service industries.

1980s' movies in particular, with their celebration of male rampage or hyper-masculinity in contention with uncaring, corrupt authority, testify to male loss of confidence rather than to what at first seems more likely, its opposite. By the 1990s, the sense of male victimization that underlies some of the most famous male rampages, those of John Rambo in particular, 'comes out'. Men find their salvation in a reassertion of sensitivity and the value that they place on family commitment. Their strengths must now be used in defence of family.

The constant tension between even hypermasculinity and feminization is signalled by, for example, the fact that spectacular heroic bodies are *spectacle* – that is, they are there to be viewed, with approving pleasure. The tension is there again in the competing claims in the 1990s of social and particularly familial responsibility, on the one hand and, on the other, heroic individualism. Laconic heroes can no longer ride off into the sunset with just a horse for company. The frontier is closed. Or else new frontiers have to be found – in space, or foreign wars – to replace the alibi for male violence that the frontier once provided.

Whatever version of masculinity is offered in Hollywood and other popular movies, one thing is certain: it is no longer unproblematic, normal, to be seen as part of nature. There is an increasing focus on masculinity as troubled and unsure of itself – never more unsure than when it is shouting its self-confidence via exaggeratedly muscular heroes toting modern weaponry.

Chapter Five
Masculinity on television

TELEVISION – A UNIQUE MEDIUM

Raymond Williams famously described the intersecting discourses of television in 1974 as 'flow'. To put this notion simply, commercial television offers programmes in bewildering succession and in juxtaposition with each other: including news of 'real events', advertisements, programme previews and station promotions. Any interruption to that flow – a break in sound and vision of beyond about ten seconds – would be felt as disturbing, drawing viewer attention to it. Such a break would perhaps have more of an impact on the viewer than any one of these constantly flowing items.

How this persuasive description of television fare as flow relates to practical criticism and to viewer experience is obscure and surprisingly little investigated. The description of spectatorship by Laura Mulvey, discussed in Chapter 3, for example, can claim some confidence about the context for its understanding of spectatorship – the cinematic apparatus. The televisual apparatus is far harder to pin down.

For example, we see films as well as 'actuality footage' on television. The difficulty of clearly separating these two sorts of viewing was recently illustrated dramatically by viewers' reception of the images of the terrorist attacks on the twin towers of the World Trade Center on September 11th, 2001. Many immediately reacted to images that were repeated and repeated throughout the length of a day on worldwide television as if they came from a particularly expensive and technologically impressive disaster movie. Perhaps this confusion was part of the psychological reaction to the unprecedented shock of the event. Surely it also provided a remarkable insight into the way that flow is difficult to sort out into discrete items. Television viewers in an obvious sense knew that what they were watching was 'actuality', and yet their initial reactions seemed to be appropriate rather to an astounding spectacle.

Williams' flow is only part of the conundrum. Television's relationship with itself is also extraordinary. It expects knowledge of it from viewers, and seems in popular programmes to refer, often humorously, to other popular programmes. In this sense, its intertextuality (the relationship of texts to one another, whereby one text references, cites or seems to quote from another) is evident. What may be unique to television, though, is the difficulty of using the term 'text' in a way that is straightforward and that instantly communicates its meaning. Television, as has been remarked, incorporates other media forms, such as movies or music videos. Further, it reruns its own programmes, and also produces decades-long soap operas, each of whose episodes makes sense only in relation to that whole (but how can we even talk of a whole when the series has not terminated and much of it remains to be written, let alone produced?).

All these factors make the study of television unusually complex. How do we answer questions about texts and viewers, when the texts are so multifarious and when we have no clear idea of how viewers consume texts? (A good example of the last point is that I am writing this section at home today, on the morning of the Brazil–England match in the quarter-final of the football World Cup. Although the TV is on in one room, I am producing the draft of this section on my laptop in another. I keep checking on the score by leaving off my work to make the short trip to glance at the television screen, but then return to my work minutes later. The fact that the television is on for the duration of the match does not mean that there is somebody watching the television screen for its duration.)

Culture critics, media and communications experts, to some extent daunted by these complex questions, still cannot afford to leave television alone. Television is an irresistible site for those who wish to chart the definitions and redefinitions of, say, gender relationships. What it seems to offer in particular is immediacy, variety, and the chance to achieve historical specificity.

GENDER STEREOTYPING AND VIEWER PERCEPTIONS

Even if the relationship of viewers with television fare is very difficult to analyse, the medium of television occupies far more of its consumers' time than any other. If images have the power to influence, which advertisers must presumably have reason to believe, then television images of masculinity surely have the potential to influence millions. Popular culture, by definition, reaches and is enjoyed by a mass of people. Nowhere is a greater mass reached than through television. It is, as Todd Gitlin puts it, 'the principal circulator of the cultural mainstream' (1987, p. 3).

For this reason, investigators of primetime television might well have felt concern in the early 1980s that males were more frequently portrayed in situations relating to their occupations than females. The latter were shown more often than men in the setting of the home, though their time divided relatively equally between home, work and other activities. Men exhibited less emotional distress than women and traditionally solved their own problems, while women were more likely to deal with the problems of others or to need help in dealing with their own. Nevertheless, one finding was very different from a similar investigation of the 1970s: that, in the later investigation, few sex differences emerged when traditional sex-typed behaviours were examined. This in particular suggested that the content of primetime television had markedly changed (Downs, 1981).

Work on gender stereotyping on television often takes children as its focus. It was concluded in 1980, for instance, as a result of work done in the 1970s, that those children who could be categorized as 'heavy viewers' had more stereotyped perceptions than 'light viewers'. Further, it was observed that stereotypic responses to male items declined with increasing age among light viewers, but were maintained with increasing age among heavy viewers. Men were perceived as more intelligent, powerful, stable and tolerant by those who maintained belief in male stereotypes. These stereotypes were deemed to be upheld in just about every aspect of television programming, including cartoons and children's programmes in general, as well as in primetime viewing (McGhee and Frueh, 1980, pp. 179–80). Not surprisingly, the lesson taken from such data was that television contributes to the acquisition of sex-stereotypic perceptions of activities and occupations thought to be appropriate to men and women.

Nearly two decades later, a national poll of American children was conducted with particular emphasis on a content analysis of television programmes, films and music videos watched by boys. The analysis suggested that men on television were represented as leaders and problem solvers. They were also depicted as funny, successful, confident, athletic and, often, focused on the opposite sex. Though they felt fear, anger, grief and pain, one-fifth of television's men used physical aggression to solve their problems. Men of colour were depicted as more likely to focus on solving problems within personal relations; by contrast, white men were depicted as principally driven by their aim to succeed at work. In relation to boys' receptiveness to stereotypes, the statistics were that 80 per cent of boys chose male personalities on television as role models, because they were 'funny'. (Interestingly, 57 per cent of girls also chose males as role models, 59 per cent females, because of their looks.) Sixty-nine per cent thought that a good description of TV males was 'angry' (CHILDREN NOW, 1999).

Other researchers have been attracted to the notion that genres are gendered – that, in other words, certain genres appeal to 'masculine' subjects (not necessarily, therefore, to men only or, for that matter, to all men), while certain others appeal to 'feminine' subjects. Examples from 1980s' television series of 'masculine' subject appeal would be *The A-Team*, of 'feminine' subject appeal, *Dynasty*.

Yet, this gendering of genres does not automatically mean that the 'messages' about gender are automatically and passively absorbed. Texts are polysemic. That is, they may be interpreted differently by different sorts of viewers (divided by ethnicity, sexuality, class, as well as gender) and in different circumstances or at different times. For this reason alone, hegemonic ideology is always to some extent under threat. There may be 'resistant' readings of texts.

Further, there is no reason to suppose that male viewers may not enjoy what dominant ideology would see as 'feminine' pleasures on offer from television (from, say, soap opera), just as female viewers may well enjoy the 'masculine' pleasures associated with cop shows. If the particular cop show happened at one time to be *Miami Vice*, something else relevant to gender discussion could be noted: a different sort of hero was presented in it. The series was one in which appearance counted for everything. This rule did not except Don Johnson, whose character did his job as a vice cop, but who was also, importantly, an overt poseur and fashion trendsetter in that show. This character was one of many TV favourites that blurred gender boundaries in a show that also muddied easy assumptions about gendered viewing.

Another factor that makes gendered genres blur common-sense gender lines is that some of them – comedies in particular – actually focus on issues of gender identity. For example, Sam Malone, the hero of *Cheers*, was characterized in a way which suggested that he was a parody of traditional male values. If the macho hero made a return in the 1980s, the impact of this was much altered by making him the butt of humour, or else having him partnered by a strong, feisty female character (as in the central couple of *Moonlighting*, played by Bruce Willis and Cybill Shepherd). Again, he might be portrayed as an anachronism, a relic of a bygone age, as with hard-boiled hero Mike Hammer.

For such reasons as these, television criticism's habit of taking gender as given, and thus unproblematic, was under serious scrutiny by the later 1980s. Many commentaries on the television medium taking gender as their principal theme seemed inadequate. Those studies, especially, which amounted to content analyses – looking at the depiction of females, for instance, in relation to an assumed cultural reality – seemed to be aiming at too narrow a target. Implicitly, they divided the world of TV representation from that of actuality, making the latter the reference point for the former. It was as if all that television did was to reflect with greater or lesser accuracy a world of real, lived gender, as if gender in life was not affected by, or even constructed by, gender in popular culture.

'MASCULINE' TELEVISION

Programmes that attempt to create and focus on a world where hegemonic masculinity holds sway share certain broad characteristics. At the most extreme, they exclude women or else represent men's importance as far exceeding that of women. The proof, as it were, of this greater importance is often located in their work. For instance, men's work is shown to underpin the economic status of their families. Additionally, men prove their worth through their work, a factor which, not coincidentally, chimes with the values of both patriarchy and capitalism.

The men of 'masculine' programming are also distinguished, by their heterosexuality, from other males grouped and characterized by their homosexuality. The late 1970s was a time when the backlash against gay rights campaigning was led by Anita Bryant in the US and by Mary Whitehouse in the UK. Again not coincidentally, it was the time when thousands of letters of protest were sent to NBC in condemnation of the openness of the representation of homosexuality in *Soap*. It might seem possible to read the greater visibility of 'gay' male and female characters in popular programmes as a sign of growing public tolerance. What severely limits the credibility of that reading is the fact that such characters, at least until the very recent *Queer As Folk,* were usually subsidiary. Moreover, the portrayal of homosexuality involved negative attributes, which were particularly so in relation to masculine identity as traditionally conceived.

All the same, so-called masculine narratives must alter if masculinity in society itself alters. (That social alteration may be significantly caused by, rather than be merely causative of, representational alteration.) Cop shows could be taken as a particularly suitable example of the masculine genre, soap opera of the feminine genre. The emphasis of one seems to be on the world of work, of the other on the domestic, the world of home. Thus, at an extreme, cop shows seem to be concerned with the public, the outdoors, toughness; soap opera with the private, the indoors, sensitivity.

Yet, this neat separation into binary opposites breaks down. We have already noted the style consciousness of *Miami Vice.* Even in this simple sense, the traditional narrative terrain of the cop-genre formula is invaded by pleasures coded as feminine – the pleasures of style, appearance and the 'look', both of the city setting and of its bonded pair of cop heroes. More significantly still, it is difficult to maintain a sense of separateness between these popular genres if attention is paid to *Hill Street Blues,* with its recognizable soap-opera tendencies.

It does not stop there, though. Soap opera itself, perhaps in a bid to maximize its appeal to a wider audience of males, perhaps also recognizing the permeability of gender, today increasingly includes themes of business, crime, violence. Possibly the soap opera's 'femininity' is retained in the way that these aspects of its plots are significantly related to personal conflict in families, between couples, between parents and children. Nevertheless, it is impossible to hold on to a rigid separation of these genres even when we note something as apparently insignificant as the fact that BBC 1's *EastEnders* sets so much of its action in the streets, particularly the open-air market area of its setting, Walford.

In the comparatively early days of television, westerns such as *Wagon Train* and *Rawhide* offered a world where men played the only important parts and where male bonding and inter-male conflict were dominant elements of the narrative. Westerns have declined in their viewer appeal on television as in movies. Where these are rerun on television, nostalgia for what is no longer to be taken for granted may explain their appeal. Nostalgia may even explain the occasional revival of the genre in such series as *Young Riders.* (This sense of nostalgia for bygone heroes of a bygone age seems to inform such movies as *Unforgiven,* with its ageing gunfighter hero played by Clint Eastwood. It was already part of the movie genre in the 1960s, notably in the comedy western *Cat Ballou,* where Lee Marvin played the broken-down has-been gunfighter character.) It is possible to extend that sense of nostalgia for the western and its world to another regretful awareness, of the passing of an era when masculinity was hegemonic, and unchallenged in its hegemony.

69

The stereotypical manhood given life by the western is still available, but more recently to children and young adults in particular. The popularity of *Teenage Mutant Ninja Turtles* at one time proves the point, with its emphasis on male bonding and on action as a means of resolution of conflict. The spirit of the western remained alive, but transported to more modern times and more up-to-date fantasies of masculinity.

One show that has been analysed as a particularly clear example from the 1980s of masculine television is *The A-Team*. The period suggests that it might be viewed as an attempt, in the decade after American defeat in Vietnam, to restore masculine authority. Class antagonism and racial difference were neutralized in the narrative in the interests of authoritarian solutions to the problems that were thrown up in each episode's story. The neutralization of working-class opposition within the narrative served the purpose of ensuring ruling-class dominance, so that the power, aggression and technology associated with restored traditional masculinity might shut down, rather than solve, conflict. Read in this way, *The A-Team* seems like a fitting entertainment for a period in which the Right was back in power, thanks to Reagan's presidency. It encapsulated the apparently popular desire to dust off and refurbish masculinity so that it might carry out what was deemed to be in the national interest.

At a more personal level, it might be suggested that men of the 1980s who were living within patriarchy could attempt to make sense of the contradictions within masculinity

Figure 5.1   The A-Team

through attention to the programme. The team as a whole embodied several of these contradictions. It acted as a composite structure, yet each of the individuals occupied a different social position and offered a particular example of the ideological construction of masculinity. In this way, *The A-Team* related to a multiplicity of social experiences of masculine life, inflected particularly by class and ethnicity. It suggested that these various experiences could be banded together to achieve male success.

The police and other agents of social authority in this series were depicted as basically stupid: heavy-handed, incapable of grasping the meaning of a challenge to that authority. It is tempting to align this comedic version of the police and the military with the assault on these perpetrated in the same decade through such immensely popular movies as *Rambo: First Blood* (see Chapter 4). In this sense, *The A-Team* represents, albeit in light-hearted mode, a form of popularly disseminated hostility to the uncomprehending, cowardly politicians and bureaucrats who lost Vietnam for the fighting man, a fantasy given wide currency through the Rambo movies in particular.

'SENSITIVE' MASCULINITY

Male sensitivity has become sufficiently accepted on television as to encompass General Schwarzkopf's public shedding of tears under the eye of the television camera. Are such signs of male emotionalism proof that after twenty years of feminism men have learned to accept their 'feminine side', or could a different sort of explanation prove more appropriate?

It is clear at least that, although there are 'unreconstructed' male characters in so-called masculine genres, exclusive attention to them from gender critics would falsify the overall picture. Part of contemporary television's representation of masculinity includes images of its 'soft' side. It is easily seen that men who never turn to violence to solve problems, who instead express their feelings and care for others, may also be characters in popular television fare. Some twenty years ago, a study of Australian television found that images of 'soft' men were common there too, designed to appeal to women, but also to men who wanted nothing to do with stereotypical machismo (Hanke, 1990, p. 233).

The appeal of 'soft masculinity' could be thought, in addition, to underlie the puncturing and parodies of conventional masculinity in sitcoms. Two popular series of the 1990s, *Home Improvements* and *Coach*, have been read by Robert Hanke as examples of what he calls the 'mock-macho sitcom' (Hanke, 1998a). The pleasure of such sitcoms can be found, he feels, in their portrayal of masculinity as a gender performance (ibid., p. 1). To this extent, queer theory's exposure of gender as performance is popularized, though it is thus clearly rendered in terms less challenging than Michel Foucault's or Judith Butler's prose.

Perhaps, though, it may be too simple to view these sitcoms as entirely undermining hegemonic masculinity. The traditional divide between the domestic sphere, characterized as part of a women's world, and the 'male' public sphere was becoming increasingly blurred by the 1990s, at least in relation to the professional white middle class. *Home Improvements* manages to make a male space within the home in which there can be 'men's talk' concerning home repair and tools, as well as discussion of wives. The sitcom's hero plays the host of a cable television show called *Tool Time*. On this show-within-a-show, solutions to problems of the home-improvement variety are macho. Yet, within the wider world of *Home Improvements*, his *Tool Time* putdowns of his wife and his unreconstructed views about gender relations, communicated to a largely male studio audience, are the subject of amusement.

At one level, the sitcom seems to ask the male viewer to get more in touch with his feminine side. Yet, it is not just pre-feminist male attitudes that are satirized here. Amusement is also created around the notion of men attempting to feminize themselves. While the show could appeal to those who are open to a critique of traditional gender roles, it is also possible to understand it as a satire about the unrealistic demands placed on any macho male who is expected to swallow his belief in hegemonic masculinity. After all, the 1990s is the decade of Robert Bly's *Iron John* (see Chapter 2). One of the basic fears expressed through that book is that boys are in danger of becoming the next generation of 'soft' men. (This danger can be averted, according to Bly, only if heterosexual men reassert their parental rights over their sons.) Within the show, the hero worries about what he sees as his sons' 'sissiness', which he tries to combat by arguing with his wife about their proper upbringing and by such direct sallies as wrestling with them in the back yard. As if to present another focus for the conflict between 'old' and 'new' males, his assistant on the cable show is targeted as the butt of insults because he represents 'soft' masculinity.

Coach, on the other hand, focuses on a 'jock' with deeply ingrained macho attitudes. The central character seems to struggle to learn new gender lessons and to overcome his deep-seated allegiance to hegemonic masculinity. To this extent, he appeals to those viewers concerned to right gender inequality. Others may justifiably detect the fakery involved in his adoption of more progressive attitudes to gender, and take pleasure in this apparent demonstration of the ineradicable nature of machismo – of machismo as, indeed, natural, something that cannot be unlearned and replaced by more 'correct' responses.

Hanke concludes that the parodies at the root of the entertainment provided by both *Home Improvements* and *Coach* enable the male viewer to move between identification and what he terms dis-identification, so that now we laugh at, now we laugh with, the heroes of these sitcoms, Tim Taylor and Hayden Fox respectively (Hanke, 1998a, p. 10).

Similar sorts of questions could be raised about audience pleasure in such earlier sitcoms as *All in the Family* and its British original, *Till Death Us Do Part*, or about that in the more contemporary British *Men Behaving Badly*. Do the jokes in, say, *Till Death Us Do Part* about unreconstructed masculinity, exposing its underlying misogyny, homophobia and racism, offer more politically aware viewers enjoyment of the exposure of hegemonic masculinity's absurdities? Or is the joke at the expense of the more politically aware and progressive within the sitcom, so that the hero's attitudes, stripped of their comic overstatement, emerge as common sense? Probably they appeal to two broad bands of viewer, by satirizing both the unreconstructed as well as the reconstructors at the same time.

This sort of observation raises a larger question, worth asking of the comedic from as early as the work of the fifth-century BC ancient Greek comic playwright, Aristophanes – is comedy basically subversive or conservative? All these sitcoms suggest that it is ridiculous for men to retain the same old attitudes to women, to homosexuality, to their own masculinity. Yet, at the same time, they could be thought merely to toy with subversive ideas to show ultimately that they too are ridiculous, and that, beneath the exaggeration and distortion, a bedrock of 'normality' remains beyond question.

Hanke's belief is that men on television and among television viewers have learned to laugh at themselves. He interprets this stance as 'neocynical', in the sense that it legitimates what he thinks of as a 'master cynicism'. In other words, for him 'these series articulate a particular discursive strategy in the sitcom "battle of the sexes", which is to reverse neocynicism (popular feminism from below) into its opposite, cynicism (the male power bloc tells the truth about themselves and denies any ability to do anything about it)' (ibid., p. 3). The parody of sitcom ends up claiming the impossibility of fundamental gender change.

A similar sort of doubt about the sensitivity apparently signalled as proper to a new conception of masculinity could be further suggested. By the early 1990s, masculine emotions, acted out publicly on television, as in the case of General Schwarzkopf's tears of sorrow, began to be taken as a mark of authenticity, of genuine feeling. Postmodernism embodies the belief that individual identity is fragmented and multiplied by contemporary culture. As Maurizia Boscagli puts it, 'In this situation, the male subject – whose position and gender prerogatives have been weakened – panics – but he is not dead' (1992–93, p. 67). According to her analysis, 'emotional masculinity' becomes a tactic whereby the male subject defends himself and his privileges. She sees the weekend retreats of the men's movement as examples of a claim of emotional authenticity. At the same time, she considers such retreats to be 'inauthentic', as examples of commodification.

Masculinity, then, can increasingly redefine itself in terms of its sensitivity, emotional expressiveness and nurturing qualities, and also in terms of its openness to improving interpersonal relations and to taking a lead part in child-rearing. However, the question is to what end this redefinition operates. A sizeable proportion of gender critics see it as largely a means to hold on to male power. Masculinity, by this understanding, becomes less hegemonic precisely in order to stay hegemonic!

73

Accordingly, the televising of male tears suggests to Boscagli both a symptom of male anxiety in a period of crisis and a particular formation of power. She notes the paradox that the postmodern male can reclaim his interiority, that he is in touch with his private emotions and his ability to express them, only if the television camera is present. His privacy must be publicly declared.

To declare publicly its interiority and intimacy, masculinity has to use some of the conventions of melodrama. Melodrama oversimplifies complex situations, rendering social and ideological conflicts in terms of the personal and the familial. It uses music to underline emotional moments, and offers tears as a mark of 'authentic feeling'. Her view is therefore: 'The logic of personalism and the valorization of interiority that characterize the contemporary masculine return to the emotions culminate in a trivialization of the ideological conflicts that produce the crisis ... of the masculine subject itself' (ibid., p. 73).

The failure of *Men* in 1989, a series centring on intimate male friendships, could be taken to indicate that this is not yet a subject welcomed by American culture outside the sitcom format (which, as we have seen above, allows for ambivalent interpretation, more reassuring to a less reconstructed public).

Part of the more sensitive version of masculinity offered by sitcoms, though, is a move away from seeing the family as the proper place for all tenderness and resolution of conflict. Once such sitcoms as *Ozzie and Harriet* eclipsed male friendships, but these reappeared in, for example, *The Honeymooners*, where the principal males expressed affection for each other and had always to make up after a fight. *The Andy Griffith Show*, centring on the life of a sheriff and his friends in a small Southern town in the USA, again prominently featured close friendship between two working-class men. The series *Give Us A Break* pivoted on an unusually affectionate relationship between a young man trying to make it as a snooker champion and his would-be manager. Both were depicted as vulnerable and emotional, able to express sorrow and joy. Helen Franks remarks of them that they didn't have to play as macho a game as football to alibi their tactile relationship with each other or their occasional embraces (1984, p. 15).

Heterosexual reassurance for such intimacy is sometimes offered by the star's persona prior to his more sensitive rendering in a sitcom. Burt Reynolds had already established his masculine credentials, as it were, before he appeared in *Evening Shade*. In the 1970s, he was one of the very first *Cosmopolitan* male nudes. Nevertheless, the context for that pin-up strongly suggested that this was a masculine joke (about the unsuitability of such a macho male in the peekaboo pose of a pin-up), however it might have been taken by buyers of the magazine. Reynolds in *The Longest Yard* and *Semi-Tough* from that same decade had established himself as a sportsman, taken to be 'playing himself' because of the evidence of his college football record. When he starred in *Evening Shade*, Reynolds' star persona enabled him to be, perhaps because his conventional masculinity was so assured, non-threatening to men and women.

In the 1980s, he had refined his movie-star image to include that of light comedian, one who was adept at mocking his own machismo – as a pose.

In *Evening Shade*, he emerged as the master of 'routine autosubeversion', in Clay Steinman's phrase (Clay Steinman, in Craig (ed.), 1992, p. 205). The show seemed to test and restore his virility, but without any resorting to physical violence. Rather, his weapons were wisecracks. His character exhibited gentleness and warmth, and relative ease with women. In some ways, this sort of masculinity comes close to suggesting that it is of the 'soft' variety. Yet, Steinman echoes the frequent doubts about its full credibility when he writes, 'more men than we might like to think might revel in the thought that Reynolds is faking it when he acts like a New Man' (ibid., p. 206).

THIRTYSOMETHING

Probably the most marked and sustained shift in US television's depiction of masculinity occurred with *thirtysomething* in the 1980s. If the decade promoted the yuppie, then *thirtysomething* was the series that dramatized the concerns of the young(ish) upwardly mobile white couple. More specifically, it focused on young male professionals of managerial status and their relations with wives, children and work.

Appearing when it did, there was more than a casual correspondence between what happened in the series and what was happening to American society within an expanding post-industrial economy. The managers of service industries often made sensitivity and caring part of their work patterns. Therapy, instead of being in a terrain outside the sphere of work, was exploited as a model for work relations. It is blatantly obvious that the men of *thirtysomething* were far less sexist than those of 'masculine' drama or 'mock-macho' sitcoms. Yet, this concentration of masculine sensitivity within the upwardly mobile middle class implicitly sent out a more negative message about male behaviour and thinking in, say, the working class or the so-called Third World. While the lives of the central couples show strains and contradictions within their ambience of caring family relationships, the picture is basically flattering to those viewers who (largely) embodied Reaganite (and, in the UK, Thatcherite) values. A better lifestyle seemed to go hand in hand with the more humane conduct of their lives along lines familiar from counselling and therapy.

Unusually, the central gender questions in the show were asked about masculinity, rather than femininity. Sasha Torres is particularly interested in the first season's credit sequences, and especially the final shot of those sequences. In it, the principal couple of the show, Hope and Michael, are spatially separated. The camera focuses on Hope holding their daughter in the nursery, but then backs out of that room and pans to Michael looking at his wife and daughter through the stair banister. Thus, the initial focus on Hope turns out to be a point-of-view shot from Michael's angle. Hope's face radiates contentment, while Michael's face is 'unreadable', suggesting a mixture of emotions. He is also less well lit than Hope, almost literally in a darker, more enigmatic place (Torres, 1989, p. 92). Torres notes that a similar effect was produced at the end of the second season's credit sequence, with Hope once again strongly suggesting maternal contentment and the shot of Michael as a contrast. Both sequences seemed to be asking the same question, '[I]n a world dominated by domesticity, where do men belong?'. As commentators of filmic melodrama have frequently claimed, critical questions about gender (here, about masculinity) are constantly being posed in the genre, but they are closed down again in surprisingly conventional manner.

The credit sequences appeared to clue the viewer in to one of the central beliefs of the series, that sexuality is a markedly different experience for males and females. Michael represented a kind of heterosexual ideal of the married man. While he desired and enjoyed sex within marriage, he was not overwhelmed by sex. Nor was he interested in extramarital sex. On the other hand, his best friend Elliot went so far as to have an extramarital affair. Michael was concerned and unhappy about this, but the series allowed a hearing for Elliot's viewpoint, that his sexual feelings could not be entirely contained within marriage. Thus, the underlying problem – that male sexuality holds out against, and cannot be contained by, bourgeois domestication – occupied an important place in the drama, but it was not ultimately dealt with and certainly not satisfactorily resolved.

Figure 5.2   Thirtysomething

One commentator, Robert Hanke, believes that what we had in *thirtysomething*'s portrayal of masculinity was a negotiated version of hegemonic masculinity. Whatever the surface appearance, we were presented with a version in complicity with dominant ideology, in that it reinforced the *status quo* of marriage and fatherhood, which could not help but foreground and privilege heterosexist assumptions (Hanke, 1990, p. 231). Once again, we seem to be back on familiar ground, where males are rendered as more sensitive, caring, and feminized precisely to maintain male privilege. Hegemonic masculinity could be thought to have been recast, rearticulated, in such series in order that within the arguably feminizing context of post-industrial capitalism its hegemony should be maintained. The rearticulation was accomplished by bringing the sexes closer in behaviour and beliefs, but also by by-passing the political and the ideological in favour of the 'personal'. That is, middle-class culture was seen as a venue where male friendship and love of family might be expressed and acted out in terms of emotional encounters and psychodramas in ways familiar from therapy.

If the series' main concern was with the self and the realization of – or failure to realize – personal happiness, it still did not entirely block out the social, political or ideological. In fact, it depicted the tensions and competitiveness involved in the world of work. It even showed relatively affluent consumers' reaction to the underprivileged in American society to the extent of a persuasive and intelligent critique of Reagan's belief in 'trickle-down'. What must also be borne in mind, though, is that all of these tensions and contradictions were ultimately seen as personal or emotional problems, to be solved within the series at the level of personal adjustment, as in therapy. This personal adjustment was so closely tied to relationships within the bourgeois family as to suggest that there was little else of real importance outside kinship and the self. For instance, it was not so much yawning social division that was addressed as whether Michael, Hope and the others could find and hold on to domestic bliss within a world that was so problematic and thus sometimes so hostile or indifferent to that happiness.

The obvious address of *thirtysomething* was to the baby boomers in their late teens up to middle life. It presented a sometimes painful but ultimately flattering image of themselves to this demographic group. Surely, though, the address must have been wider. Presumably it must have touched on the same hopes and aspirations that President Reagan reached through the rhetoric of the 1980s. If the yuppie lifestyle was not exactly within the grasp of some of the viewers, surely the dream that it represented in the series did not seem so much a remote fantasy as an achievable reality with the right attitude to work and to life.

We have already noted that, however 'soft' and feminized *thirtysomething*'s approved version of middle-class masculinity was, it was implicitly heterosexist if only for making its central reality and hope for fulfilment the middle-class heterosexual family of husband, wife and children.

WILL AND GRACE

What, then, of the contemporary sitcom, *Will and Grace*, with its domestic pairing of a confused, but clearly heterosexual, career woman and a happy, and homosexual, lawyer? All of this is set in the context of a sophisticated Manhattan of witty repartee and of basically caring – but extra-familial and seldom sexual – relationships. Since the series seems to invite empathy with and understanding of socially marginalized sexualities and lifestyles, it would at first sight seem to be laying to rest the long-standing privileging of heterosexual family men as exemplars of sensitive masculinity.

Perhaps this may be to overstate the ideological shift suggested at some level by *Will and Grace*. Noticeably, for example, Will (Eric McCormick) plays off a far more flamboyant and stereotypically gay, camp stereotype Jack (Sean Hayes). It would seem that Will manages to be a sympathetic lead character by embodying – all the more sharply by this contrast – a surprisingly 'normal' version of white middle-class male homosexuality. Will does occasionally express sexual attraction to another male, but this is usually conceived and depicted along lines that a heterosexual female would experience in a sitcom. Male/male courtship – and courtship itself is a feature of conventionalized heterosexual romance – is conducted via expensive, candle-lit dinners, for example. The personality of the party in whom Will is interested counts for far more than his sexual allure. Once again, the conventions of heterosexual romance, as filtered through the world of sitcom, appear to dominate. Although Will's masculinity is to some extent ensured by marking it off from Jack's, it resembles that of a successful career woman rather than that of a materially secure, good-looking, sexually adventurous and less relationship-oriented, young homosexual male loose in New York City.

As so often in mainstream entertainment, homosexuality is welcomed, provided it is conceived in terms that make it a form of heterosexuality or, more accurately, female heterosexuality, at one remove. Camp stereotypes have long had a warm welcome from straight audiences. Will is seldom depicted as such. He is a perfect companion for Grace, sharing some of her personal goals to the extent of being attracted sometimes to the same man, with at least the appearance of more masculine confidence. This confidence can be converted to a nurturing of Grace when she is disappointed in love or unhappy with her life. In a sense that would be widely recognized within lesbian/gay subculture, Will and Grace are 'girlfriends'. If this is so, then the old adamantine link between male heterosexuality and popular conceptions of masculinity is reconfirmed rather than questioned.

CLASS, ETHNICITY AND SOCIAL STATUS

Stanley Aronowitz, in 1992, argues that from the mid-1970s there were no direct representations of working-class males – or of working-class females – on television. Working-class representation tended to be relocated to the world of beer commercials, or concentrated in the ghetto of the cop show. In this latter sort of series, he believes that the characteristics of working-class culture found a new context, that of the stationhouse and the bars where the police went to relax between bouts of duty (Aronowitz, 1992, pp. 204–5).

Hill Street Blues often featured the discussion of personal problems, both domestic and professional in nature. Nevertheless, this discussion would be between cop partners. The 'family' of the police became a setting in which problems attendant on the relations of sex and gender could be worked out. Class solidarity was explored through the tensions between the cops and their captain, or regular cops and lieutenants with authority invested in them. Masculinity was softened by being open to discussion, the laconicism of the sole vigilante sort of cop being replaced by conversation between trusted partners. Yet, class in this sort of generic context replaces sex and gender or else alibis these.

Part of the effect of male bonding in class terms is the bypassing of ethnicity as a significant factor. The closeness of Robert Culp and Bill Cosby in *I Spy* was never qualified by the characters' skin colours. Race questions are largely off television's agenda. They were not allowed to be raised by, for example, *The Cosby Show*, which by featuring a world of black middle-class affluence and 'respectability' managed to suggest a world in which affirmative action was scarcely even relevant.

This is not to say that certain television shows from the 1970s, and even possibly the 1960s also, failed to question the values of popular television culture – those associated with the middle-class nuclear family, the rightness of patriotism, the unquestionable naturalness of hegemonic masculinity. Such series as *The Mary Tyler Moore Show*, *All in the Family* and *M*A*S*H* were among those commercially successful series that asked such questions of hitherto largely unquestionable depictions.

Postmodernism, which is sometimes most clearly exemplified with reference to television entertainment, by its nature shakes up the conventional – if only by exposing to viewing audiences that something *is* a convention that, by being exposed as such, can no longer be viewed with the same easy assumptions.

A principal feature of postmodern culture is the lessening of emotional connection between viewer and viewed. The artworks of Andy Warhol today stand as one of the best exemplifications of that claimed aspect. Many of his portraits are just a series of images, which suggest that there is no more profound reality behind the series. Marilyn Monroe in Warhol's work is no less a manufactured image than a labelled tin of Campbell's soup. This idea of lack of affect (emotional connection) and lack of substance in imagery is illustrated particularly well by television's *Miami Vice*, where Crockett and Tubbs did not so much look at one another as stare past each other, connecting as little in their emotions as in their words. When Crockett did experience emotion, as when he fell for a woman who would, inevitably in this context, prove false and dangerous to him, it was a trap. His way of rising above the risk that emotional connection represented to him was to adopt attitudes, clothes, 'mirror shades'. *Miami Vice*'s concern with surface and look, both at a human level and that of the cityscape, replaced the customary sorts of response to personal, psychological probing in different sorts of cop series.

TELEVISION'S SHIFTING PATTERNS

The discussion above suggests that neither television entertainment itself nor the representation of masculinity on TV is a monolith. It shifts with the social – not surprisingly, since television's output is part of the social and has effects on it as well as being affected by it. The difficulty is to avoid being so impressed with the many surface changes and shifts as not to notice what remains constant. Another difficulty is, conversely, to avoid being so impressed with what remains constant as not to notice the many changes and shifts.

One development in television representation that needs to be kept in mind is the way that the workplace is reconceived even in the 1970s. From this point, the workplace is conceptualized as not so much a contrast with the family home as an area where displaced elements of the familial resurface in disguised form.

The stability suggested as an essential part of family life in sitcoms of the 1950s and 1960s, for example, is rediscovered in different form in the workplace at a time when domestic togetherness seems to become more of a social ideal than an actuality. The cop heroes of *Starsky and Hutch* were bonded by the nature of their work. Yet, they passed time together, sharing emotional support for each other, in a way that began to suggest that work could supply what the domestic setting sometimes failed to offer. A similar phenomenon was noticeable in the female-cop series, *Cagney and Lacey*.

The return to more conservative right-wing values in American politics under President Reagan in the 1980s had men continuing to bond with each other in a way that they did not with women. (*The A-Team* and *Magnum, P.I.* both placed a value on easy male homosociality that was not matched by sexual relationships, which were depicted as largely superficial or short-lived.) Precipitate conclusions about male representation in 1980s television could be simplistic, however. As *thirtysomething* demonstrates, the 1980s is also the decade in which more vulnerable men were shown, aware of difficulties in their marriages and their workplaces alike, and talking with each other about these.

Perhaps part of the explanation for shifts in male TV representation, particularly those showing men as less macho than in westerns or earlier cop shows, could be sought in viewing figures. Women are known to have been an important target audience by the 1980s. Feminism might have helped bring about a new openness to and valuing of male intimacy, but also the desire to bring in more female viewers to hitherto male genres should be given due weight as explanation. Then, too, male viewers uninterested in the constant repetition of male machismo might have been persuaded to take a new interest in a show which gave a prominent place to male intimacy.

What could be seen as an increasing feminization of the male hero, even of cop shows, is given renewed emphasis when it is recognized that Tom Selleck, as Magnum, became an obvious example of the eroticized male object, in his high-cut shorts, easy awareness of his appeal and his directing of masculine charm towards the camera. No less was Sonny, the Don Johnson character of *Miami Vice*, an erotic object. The redressing of this 'feminization' by such culturally masculine attributes as facial stubble and laconic toughness of personality as a cop surely simply proved the aware-ness of the series' writers and producers of this facet of this particular cop show. They needed an alibi with which to negotiate the dangers of too unrelieved feminization.

Even when they were not attracting viewers to their TV shows with their faces, bodies and accoutrements, the heroes of such primetime viewing as *Dallas* and *Dynasty* in the 1980s showed an appreciation of women's interests and desires within these soap operas. Accompanying the seemingly more aware and responsive male hero was the more frequently featured 'strong woman' heroine, whether that be highly self-assertive Joan Collins as Alexis in *Dynasty*, or Cybill Shepherd as the wise-cracking, clear-sighted counterpart to Bruce Willis's hero in *Moonlighting*.

As if to unsettle this emerging picture of shifts in 1980s television's representation of gender, some took the primetime TV season of 1985–86 as a time of the rebirth of the macho man as a backlash against the more sensitive male of then recent seasons.

Figure 5.3 Miami Vice

Evidence of this belief was claimed to be found in Sam Malone as the unrecon-structed ex-sportsman hero of *Cheers*, or Willis's 'hard-boiled' David Addison in *Moonlighting*.

Nevertheless, to show that this picture was itself an oversimplification, it must be pointed out that there had never been an absence of unreconstructed males in main roles – Archie Bunker, for instance, from *All in the Family* in the 1960s, and J. R. Ewing from *Dallas*, were hardly 'new men'. Furthermore, Sam Malone's male-chauvinist attitudes were expected to provoke laughter, difficult as that laughter could prove to interpret. David Addison might be more fairly taken not so much as hard-boiled as brash.

There are other ways of looking at television in the 1980s than as simply the decade of a shift in the direction of feminizing the male, or alternatively as one which attempted to halt that change by a revival of the macho male. It may well be that these are but two of the strands which combined to show that the conflict between old and new gender roles was being fought out repeatedly, in programme after pro-gramme – suggesting different resolutions and even different winners to different members of the viewing public.

TWO RECENT EXAMPLES

SIX FEET UNDER

The seemingly dysfunctional southern California family at the centre of this series happens to own an undertaking business. It is highly unusual for entertainment to focus on death. Yet, every episode of this series begins with its 'death of the week' and ends in a dazzling white light which suggests the transition of souls to another realm. It is practically taboo for death (perhaps more accurately 'the death business') to be treated satirically. Here undertaking, with its attendant skills of grief counselling, is seen to be part of the business world, complete with tacky commercials for embalm-ing fluid and funeral supplies. Perhaps because Alan Ball, the writer of *American Beauty*, has created a family in crisis in the midst of extreme grief and horror, the fam-ily's masculinities are explored with almost unprecedented candour.

In the first few minutes of the pilot episode, the paterfamilias is killed. Instead of rep-resenting the Freudian focal point, he remains an enigma in death, of uncertain rele-vance to the lives of his wife and children. He subsequently appears to the various individuals of his family while they are in shock. At one point, he even sits wryly observing one son making love with his policeman boyfriend.

The guilt, secretiveness and grim sense of duty in the gay son are contrasted with the relative openness, emotionality and affection of the once absent brother. The latter is recognizably more 'in touch with his feminine side'. He empathizes more easily with women: his repressed, yet sexually alive mother, his neurotic sister and his neurotic girlfriend. The son whom tradition might have characterized as more feminine flees intimacy, choosing one-night stands over the love of a policeman, again characterized against tradition as caring, generous-hearted and accepting of his sexual orientation.

Death – that of the father, those of so many strangers – seems to dissolve the world of bourgeois, suburban 'normality' so that the family has to face weekly facets of itself which might have been reserved in less extreme situations for the televisual equivalent of a third act. It seems almost to substantiate queer theory's refusal to accept societal belief in the reality of patriarchal, nuclear-family masculinities (and femininities).

MALCOLM IN THE MIDDLE

This sitcom, like such other Fox Network examples as *The Simpsons* or *Married with Children*, is in its own way as subversive of expectations about representation of the nuclear family as *Six Feet Under*. Judged by the standards of earlier family sitcoms, the Wilkersons are almost as dysfunctional as the funeral-business family, if in a less spectacular ways. Again, they prove no less able, paradoxically, to survive, function and progress.

Three Wilkerson sons live at home – Malcolm (Frankie Muniz) being in the middle in terms of age – while a fourth, Francis, uses his devious talents in the ambience of an insanely run military academy. Each of the home-living sons possesses a different talent for survival: the eldest, Reese, uses aggression in the playground and unashamed stupidity at home; the youngest, Dewey, has the face and quirky unflappability of an infant Buster Keaton; Malcolm, often embarrassed to have been identified as academically gifted, survives on his wits. Unlike the other family members, he will confide his private thoughts to the TV audience, and yet his insights are not detached and objective. He remains in character in his observations.

The father is hardly a paterfamilias. He is depicted as a barely disguised child himself, one who often joins in his boys' scams and tomfoolery. He is so atypical as a represented father that he alone of the family feels warm affection for his counterpart among the newly arrived, and troublesome, next-door neighbours. When they leave and a new family takes their place, the new father leans over the fence to greet Mr Wilkerson. 'It's too soon', the latter explains, almost tearfully, as he retreats.

Along with the collapse of the father's traditional masculinity is the pseudo-matriarchal tyranny exercised over every male in the family by the mother. She exceeds all of her family in their particular version of masculinity: more aggressive than Reese, more shrewd than Malcolm, Francis or their father, sufficiently attuned to Dewey's whims to anticipate them. Politicians of the Right sometimes publicly hanker after a revival of the sitcom family of yore. The Wilkersons and the Simpsons seem to recognize that they can offer the public a more persuasive version. In so doing, they also offer a set of masculinities that are both deromanticized and appealing to many viewers. These masculinities are far from hegemonic.

Figure 5.4   Malcolm in the Middle

IN CONCLUSION

It is noticeable that the 1980s has been a decade of particular appeal to television critics taking gender – and especially masculinity – as their brief. This seems to be primarily because the popular culture represented by television in that period can with most clarity be linked with the socio-political context of American life. There is, after all, a striking change in the US political scene in 1980, with Ronald Reagan's Republican presidency taking over from Democrat Jimmy Carter's. Profound economic change was already occurring in the later 1970s, with the shift to service industries, and the consequent shaking up of the marketplace. The peculiar relevance to masculinity of this is illustrated by the realization that men could no longer expect a job for life, or that they, rather than their wives, should be the family breadwinners. Yet another problem for masculinity was American loss of confidence in traditional notions of militarism and patriotism after the nation's defeat in Vietnam. Part of President Reagan's brief seemed to be a turning round of US social experience, which involved a reinterpretation of the past, one which permitted hegemonic masculinity to be dusted off and polished up afresh, in the spheres of family life, patriotism and sexuality. This president seems to have been peculiarly aware of the value of the popular for a fresh configuration of the US and its values.

Some sort of popular salve for vastly changed gender relations was likely to have been sought in television's representations and myths. Susan Jeffords has been particularly fascinated by Rambo movies and similar depictions of male heroism in the light of Reagan's project, outlined immediately above. Many academics have followed her lead, but in the sphere of television. Here, they notice the resurgence of hegemonic masculinity (in, for example, *The A-Team*), but they also have to deal with the apparent paradox that 'soft' masculinity and sensitive heroes are so frequent and popular, especially in sitcoms of the 1980s, but also in its cop shows and the yuppie melodrama, *thirtysomething*.

Perhaps the paradox, they suggest, is more apparent than real. Popular culture is strongly aware that masculinity is no longer to be taken for granted, as normal or natural. Too much has happened to it in the 'real world' for it simply to be reasserted unquestioned. Hence, when it is apparently reasserted, it is often within the world of sitcom, where laughter is invited for machismo. This raises questions about whether the laughter is subversive or confirmatory in effect, and suggests the possibility that it is both.

The focus on television of the 1980s should not blind us to the probability that the decade, from one understanding of it, merely offers particularly useful insights into processes that have been there since the 1950s and certainly continue today. In terms of male representation, popular television has both to respond to historical change and to find ways of inflecting its accounts so that social ideals of hegemonic masculinity receive recognition. The popular audience is given choice, the broadest being to see machismo as an undeniable component of successful male personality or as an embarrassing anachronism. As with so many apparently stark choices offered by popular culture, the viewer may not only opt for one or other, possibly at different times and in different moods, but may take both. This probable scenario, when applied at various times and in the context of various media, gives us remarkable insight into the ways that not only television, but wider popular culture, operates – and precisely how, indeed, it manages to stay popular.

Chapter Six

Masculinity in advertising

GENDER STEREOTYPING IN ADVERTISING

A great deal of the public anxiety about the influence of television images upon children concerns violence. Some researchers, nonetheless, have been primarily interested in children's acquisitions of ideas about gender from television in general, and from television commercials in particular.

As has been touched on in Chapter 5, there is difficulty in making confident claims about the nature of television-watching. Because a television is on for lengthy periods in the home, it does not mean that it is being watched intently or even at all for that entire time. There is increasing recognition that we know little of how viewers watch the medium. It is hard to be certain whether, for instance, commercials are given the same attention by viewers as programmes, or whether the commercial break is taken as a break in attention span or even a break from viewing.

Nevertheless, there seems to be wide consensus that, to judge from children's viewing in particular, more exposure to mass media in general means more sex-typed views of the world. (This is obviously a more likely conclusion if the more influential mass media portray stereotyped sex roles.) The consensus among researchers seems to be that this applies to both genders of young viewer, and that 'heavy' television viewing produces a decrease in educational aspirations together with an increase in sexist attitudes. Perhaps, though, it is fairer, rather than to think of an 'increase' (which implies that children's views are already relatively fixed), to notice the important role that observation of mass-media models plays in the process of children's learning of sex differences in behaviour.

Researchers into the social effects of television-watching are united in believing that the medium takes up a highly significant total of time. In the mid-1970s, for example, it was reckoned by Leslie Zebrowitz McArthur and Beth Gabrielle Resko that television reaches 95 per cent of American homes and, more strikingly, that 64 per cent of the 'average pre-schooler's' time would be spent watching television – more than in the classroom during four years of college. These same researchers calculated that 20 per cent of air time was devoted to commercials (McArthur and Resko, 1975, p. 210). In 1988, it was concluded that the so-called average American watched 714 commercials per week, or over 37,000 per year (Bretl and Cantor, 1988, p. 596).

Advertising is probably at its most unrelenting in the area of television commercials, whether or not the 20 per cent figure cited above is a fair estimate for their share of air time. For that reason, social-science research into the links between advertising and gender beliefs focuses significantly on television commercials, particularly on the belief that these have a crucial influence on the very young and that this influence must carry on into adult life.

Content analyses of 1970s' television commercials noted largely that men and women were portrayed in stereotypical roles – typically, women in commercials were home-makers, men involved in the pursuit of careers; the former were unintelligent and sub-missive, the latter intelligent and independent. Such readings of the portrayal of gender were strengthened by research into advertising in 'general-interest magazines'. Only minor changes seemed to have occurred within their advertisements over a 20-year period, according to a 1983 publication (Courtney and Whipple, 1983, p. 4). Men were once again more likely than women to be performing work outside the home. They were also more likely to be involved in the purchase of more expensive goods and services. While women in 1970s' advertising were usually portrayed as central to the promotion of domestic products, men were central to that of alcohol, cars and business products.

The degree to which advertising in the 1980s kept to or broke away from the gender stereotyping discerned in the 1970s is a matter of contention. Some researchers see few signs of change from one decade to the next. Others conclude that there is sig-nificantly new emphasis in the increasing depiction of people without reference to family – shown alone and in close-up. The point of this absence of family or other social context has clear relevance to allowing a wider variety of potential consumers to identify with the subject position. All the same, social effects are arguable: that the opening out of gendered portrayals beyond work and family served to weaken the link between stereotypical representation and social belief in stereotypes.

One potentially interesting development in this sort of research was a growing aware-ness that there are differences among various societies' advertising, and that these could be seen as more or less encouraging of stereotyping. Thus, it has been claimed that, while UK commercials were similar to the US variety in this respect, Mexican commercials were the most heavily stereotypical with regard to gender. By way of con-trast, Australian commercials were less stereotyped in the matters of occupation and marital status or in the apparent credibility of both female and male spokespersons for a product (Gilly, 1988, p. 75).

The representation of the male in the 1990s appears to be sharply differentiated from that of the preceding two decades. Contempt for men, in such diverse terms as their emotional shallowness, lack of common sense, incompetence in the domestic setting, unattractiveness of appearance and personality in the morning, has become sufficiently frequent in advertising as to be remarkable precisely because it seems to be taken as so unremarkable! Possibly allied with this is the relative frequency of the male as sex object in such apparently unisexed contexts as that for Lee jeans or Coca-Cola. As Rosalind Coward puts it, men's 'sexual humiliation by women is now a stand-ard part of advertising's rhetoric' (1999, p. 90).

It has to be said about the preceding survey of research into gender stereotyping in television commercials, as well as other contexts, that some of it would be seen today as over-confident in its assumptions and conclusions. In particular, there has often been a blurring of the lines between 'sex' and 'gender'. Then, too, just as in the world of movie representation, it might be worth considering that masculinities should be seen as multiple and even contradictory. Some of this multiplicity would appear to need to be tied in with such other representations as those of class or ethnicity, for instance.

If these provisos have validity, then some of the research into what is believed to be sex stereotyping might be accused of oversimplifying and making unwarranted generalizations. Much of it is also a matter of content analysis. What has been omitted by it is the question of how representation takes place, with what relation to the viewer. It seldom asks how legitimate it is to take for granted that what is apparently said of the gendered world in advertising applies common-sensically to the socially gendered world of consumers.

MASCULINITY AS REPRESENTED IN ADVERTISING

THE VISUAL

One of the ways of determining whether a male character in an advertisement has the required authority and suggests the appropriate power is through visual appearance. His strength may be suggested not only in terms of his physique, but also in the suggestion of his affluence and business success. The myth of masculine independence is embodied in confident and confidence-inspiring appearance.

However, this latter aspect may be connoted by the late 1980s – sometimes a business suit alone can suggest it: 'what he [the male imaged by advertising] definitely does not want, and goes to some measure to avoid, is to appear less than masculine, in any way weak, frilly, feminine' (Barthel, 1988, p. 175). By the 1990s, men's visual representation frequently suggested danger or, say, the strength lurking beneath the uniforms of American football players, or in boxers and bikers. This trend is particularly obvious in the commercials inserted in major sporting events as televised in the US, in that the military is promoted, as well as weight-training machines and nutritional supplements. This sort of advertising suggests its distinct separation from the more androgynous masculinity associated with, for example, fashion advertisements.

Visual change could suggest change in social beliefs about men. Shifts in visual representation of masculinity were already happening, in less extreme forms, prior to the 1990s. It has, however, already been suggested above that the 1990s ushers in a period when men and masculinity are openly ridiculed. Something that may help to explain this, and at the same time to make sense of the way the male body is regularly objectified erotically in advertising, is a possible awareness that culture has been feminized by consumerism. A consumer society may grow to see itself as submissive and easily manipulated, and thus to see its males as occupying the position that was once attributed exclusively to the female.

It is more likely in recent advertising that the purchase of particular consumer goods by the male will result in female attention to him. This provides a clear contrast with the advertising world of the 1980s' and 1990s', where the male's authority preceded the promotion of a product, so that that product might be recommended to other, presumably less confident, men or to women. Or perhaps advertising does not simply attest to the feminization of both men and women. It is possible to read *Esquire* advertisements of the 1980s', for instance, as indicating a growing toughness and confidence in women. Paradoxically, this could make the men of these advertisements the more masculine – because they are not intimidated by such assertive women (Kervin, 1990, p. 67).

MASCULINITY AND THE DOMESTIC

As early as 1967, two researchers into the portrayal of American men and women in television commercials noted that the attributes of masculinity – such as muscularity, knowledgeability, dominance, independence, athleticism, aggression – work as such only if the male is kept out of the domestic setting and away from his family. Once the American male is seen as a father or husband, his judgments appear to be limited to the ability to recognize good coffee. In the domestic setting, he loses his independence and self-assured nature and, as son or spouse, welcomes nurturing and overprotection. Thus, the American male, swift as a panther, free as a mustang outside the home, is infantilized within the family, becoming stupid and emasculated. It is concluded, 'For men there are ... dreams of power and raw violence, as well as a return to the protection of a nurturant mother' (Bardwick and Schumann, 1967, p. 23).

Interestingly, such a conclusion suggests not only that traditional hegemonic masculinity is seriously compromised by the comforts of home, but that there is strong appeal to men in the notion of trading in such masculinity for the mothering provided by their wives and mothers in a wishful domestic setting.

MEN AS AUTHORITATIVE/DOMINANT

In 1975, McArthur and Resko claimed that 70 per cent of males in the American television commercials they had sampled were portrayed as authorities, with only 30 per cent portrayed as product users. This contrasted with 14 per cent of females as authorities, 86 per cent as product users (McArthur and Resko, 1975, p. 214).

Later research has some bearing on this finding, Brownlow and Zebrowitz, in a 1990 investigation into the relation in television commercials of credibility to appearance, concluded that, while women were portrayed as less expert than men, they were depicted as more trustworthy, regardless of age, attractiveness and amount of smiling: 'males delivered communications that were more expert and less trustworthy than those delivered by females ... [which] corresponds to the sex stereotype that males are more logical and objective' (Brownlow and Zebrowitz, 1990, p. 58).

Certain products, if we extend this line of argument, appear to lend themselves better to promotion by appeal to masculine authority. One distinction suggested as germane to understanding the different genders' employment in advertising contexts derives from John Berger's belief that men create a sense of identity by extending out from their body to control objects and other people. By contrast, women work with and within the body. The former conception seems to be relevant to male promotion of certain kinds of product – notably in car advertisements and those for alcohol and stereos (Barthel, 1988, p. 8).

Harris and Stobart, working in 1986 on the matter of sex-role stereotyping in British television advertisements, took particular interest in the times of day when stereotyping seemed to be intensified. Thus, in the daytime, it was females who took a more dominant role, advancing rational and fact-based arguments, with men offering mere opinions. This pattern was reversed in the evenings (Harris and Stobart, 1986, p. 162). An obvious suggestion from their work is that the gender of authority figures shifts according to demographic trends in the television audience. Whether or not, in a period of high unemployment in the UK, daytime television audiences were largely or exclusively female, the belief seems to have been that they were. Therefore, the dominant gender, interpreted as such in relation to authoritativeness of pronouncement, may be female in daytime television, but not when men are reckoned to be a significant element, as in evening viewing. The dominance of a particular gender in commercials' portrayals of men and women would appear to be directly related to the perceived dominance of a particular gender in the social word of television viewing.

Given this probability, it is no surprise to learn that, in advertisements aimed at boys, they are portrayed as more active, aggressive and rational, thus more dominating, than girls (Fejes, in Craig (ed.), 1992, p. 14).

VOICEOVERS AND GENDER

Particular interest has been paid by some research into television commercials and gender to the way that voiceovers have been distributed among male and female voices, as well as to the sorts of meaning that can be read into this distribution. Broadly, it could be argued that the male voiceover is taken to be saying something rational and objective, thus undeniably true. The female voiceover, however, has a distinct appeal, and not only to other women. It is associated with nurturing, maternal qualities, to promise something that is good for one and probably, in addition, emotionally satisfying.

To see the female voiceover as appropriate for a listener of inferior status to that of a person listening to masculine rationality may thus be to oversimplify. Even the tying of gendered voices to particular products may not be as unchanging as it once seemed to be. At one time, the dominant voice in food commercials was female. No longer, though. Can this change really be due only to the fact that 1980s' advertisements sometimes chose to have men eating at fast-food venues, as one commentator suggests (Lovdal, 1989, p. 721)?

On the evidence up to the end of the 1980s, it would seem, however, as if advertisers generally much prefer the narrator's voice to be authoritative and thus, it appears, male. Whatever the precise thinking, no less than 90 per cent of all US television commercials' narrators were male up to 1988. In British television commercials for that decade, a similarly overwhelming domination by the male voiceover is claimed. Male authoritativeness can be seen by some as a feature inherent in the voice, but it is surely more convincing to take the male voice as signifying authority because in general terms the male is seen as the more authoritative sex in society. The cultural interpretation of the male voiceover helps to explain why the male is an authority figure even in commercials apparently addressed to women viewers. (A general exception to this pattern sometimes occurs, however, when the items being promoted are classifiable as 'women's products'.)

MASCULINITY IN 1990s' ADVERTISING

Before the 1990s', it seemed to be the case that only men had sufficient sense of humour to show it in advertisements. One notable change in the 1990s has been indicated above: men as objects of contempt, sometimes even when they are presented as erotic objects. This change has entailed the deriding of men by women and, to that extent, since the contempt is always expressed ironically or as a joke, at least the attribution of wit or humour to female characters.

The prevalence of 1990s' advertising's men as, in Laura Mulvey's coinage, 'to-be-looked-at' means not only that their pretensions to sexual allure can be themes for caustic female comments but, increasingly today, that male narcissism is presented straight, as it were, and not defensively disavowed by humour. Sean Nixon has pointed out that the significance of 'new man' imagery is not merely in terms of a freeing up of traditional gender confines – the eroticism of male appearance also means that the traditional oppositions of sexualities between men identifying as straight or as gay have been considerably loosened (Nixon, 1996, p. 202). Eroticization of the male appearance, relatively commonplace in 1990s' advertising, is taken by him to begin with Nick Kamen's undressing to his underpants in the 1950s' launderette, in the famous commercial which ran from Boxing Day 1985 to autumn 1986. He allies with the relative passivity and objectification of Kamen a new softness and sensuality coded through his lips, eyes and skin tone.

The to-be-looked-at male in more recent advertisements seems to be put in the position of the commonly eroticized female of previous years. All the same, Nixon agrees with Frank Mort that the new imagery of men spoke particularly to men through their gender, as part of a community of men, recognizing the less monolithic, more provisional nature of masculinity (ibid., p. 4).

Another, possibly allied, alteration beginning in the later 1980s is advertising's stress on pleasure rather than work as integral to consumption. Yet, it may be that work, while invisible, is being addressed in a curiously subliminal way. If consumption is linked with pleasure, the means by which products are acquired and consumed is getting ahead (through work). This sort of reasoning helps us to understand that the more obvious message of 1990s' advertising – that gender and lifestyle are conceived in new, less traditional ways – masks another, more likely, explanation: 'the impetus behind much … non-traditional coding is not a celebration of stereotypical gender traits being supplanted, but rather advertising's continuing need for a new means to capture and hold the consumer's attention' (Kervin, 1990, p. 68).

Advertising's need to capture and hold the consumer's attention is a useful explanation also for the fact that what it represents is not a single masculinity, but masculinities in the plural. Particular target audiences for advertisements may well have vastly differing conceptions of what is most desirable as masculine (or feminine) traits. Sensitivity seems, for example, to be valued much more highly as a masculine trait among women than among men. Then, too, because cultural conventions alter over time, cultural constructions of gender must also change. Gender is a dynamic construct, which is unlikely in representation to be tied down to a fixed version of the various possibilities.

Nevertheless, there are areas of advertising where there seems to be investment in a particularly traditional set of beliefs about masculinity. It is to this sort of advertising that attention will be directed in the following instances.

BEER COMMERCIALS

The version of masculinity which is harnessed for the selling of beer in 1980s' US commercials is one which banishes emotionality, along with sensitivity and thoughtfulness. Instead, images of male solidarity are offered. A community of men, coded as uniformly heterosexual, is envisioned, in which boys are initiated into manhood through the acquisition of the ability to drink beer. Manhood is linked with challenge, risk and with mastery over challenges from nature, technology and other men.

In the presumed belief that the target audience for beer commercials is largely male and that images of hegemonic masculinity will produce the most positive response, beer advertisers assemble a kind of rulebook for appropriately masculine behaviour. Their 30-second commercial spots in combination produce a guide to the characteristics of what seems to be the man's man. The setting of these commercials' is often the outdoors when, that is, it is not the bar. By this means, it is not just that the drinking of beer is rendered a natural activity, where men at least are concerned, so that the beverage becomes water from a mountain stream. Rather, masculinity, which beer-drinking represents in this context, freed from the constraints of mundane civilization, is itself part of nature.

The common denominator of working hard and then playing hard, albeit playing boyishly, is found across a range of masculine types. Lance Strate, who views beer commercials as, in his words, a manual on masculinity, has usefully collected examples. Thus, Busch beer commercials specialize in the portrayal of cowboys riding horses, performing in rodeos, driving cattle. Budweiser uses blue-collar, along with a small selection of white-collar, workers: lumberjacks, construction workers, soldiers. Miller Genuine Draft prefers farm hands and piano movers. Strate understands the work that is an important part of all this imagery as an integral part of man's identity. It is work offered for the benefit of family and nation, but it is also linked with pride in accomplishment, and the desire to earn the respect and ensure the camaraderie of other men (Strate, in Craig (ed.), 1992, p. 80).

These commercials both select from, but also reinforce and augment, the mythology of the masculine available in wider American culture. If work is an assertion of man's ability to triumph over the challenges of nature and technology, leisure is conceived of as the result of that work. The reward for hard work is winning the esteem and companionship of other men. While leisure time is the period where other men can express their respect and camaraderie, it is often also an occasion for men's demonstration of mastery over nature and each other, through the symbolic challenges of pool or even those of professional sports, which men watch on the bar-room's TV.

Figure 6.1

The bar itself is as welcoming and relaxing as the central location of the then contemporary television sitcom *Cheers*. Bartenders and waitresses are friendly and glad to serve the clients. Strate points out that nobody ever pays for their drinks, either literally or in the longer term, in the sense of suffering consequences for all this beer-drinking (ibid., p. 85).

Marlboro advertisements exploit imagery of masculine self-reliance and independence. Beer commercials depend, however, on images of masculine homosociality. In other words, they feature men who are always in the company of other men. The cohesiveness of the group is paramount, so that competitiveness, while potentially present, is played down. One-to-one relationships are avoided, except occasionally for a father/son duo. The humour that was noted above as a peculiarly masculine trait in 1980s' advertising in general reappears here. An explanation is suggested both for humour in this context and possibly more widely for its strong association with masculinity elsewhere: it is a lubricant for interaction among males, one which manages, however, to avoid emotional display and which suggests restraint at the same time as male affection.

Where women do make an appearance in the almost exclusively male world of the beer commercials' bar-room, they are conceived generally as an admiring audience for the male beer-drinker and for the feats which he is called on to perform. Cool detachment is positively valued in the man. His interest in a woman must not be so absorbing as to distract him from the beer. She does not resent his drinking, his commitment to male companionship or his coolness in her presence. She is represented in terms of the admiring good sport. One 1970s' UK advertisement epitomized these attitudes by giving the blowsy barmaid this line after she has tried the drink for herself: 'No, too strong for me – but I like the men who drink it.'

CAR ADVERTISEMENTS

Todd Gitlin has analysed the sorts of car commercial widely in circulation during the 1980s', the decade of Reaganism. The man at the centre of these car commercials is reminiscent of a pilot, a driver who soars unimpeded through or above obstacles. He is, for Gitlin, the embodiment of a master fantasy of the Reagan era, a man on the move, untouched by the messiness of the everyday. The fantasy is one 'of thrusting, self-sufficient man, cutting loose, free of gravity, free of attachments' (Gitlin, in Gitlin (ed.), 1987, p. 143). He sees this less as futuristic than as an updating of the persistent American myth of the frontiersman – a hunter, trapper, cowboy riding through wide open spaces, with no responsibility to anybody other than to make life safe for more domesticated, weaker settlers.

The modern version does not feel this latter sense of responsibility, however. In late-twentieth-century terms, the lone driver is conceived as a high-performance professional. Part of Reaganite economic belief was the concept of trickle-down, whereby the high flier, by self-enrichment, also benefited the weaker in society by spending and donating more to them. The refurbishing of the frontiersman image is effected in Reaganite entrepreneurial terms. He is the official cultural hero whose enrichment is 'to everyone's good and at no one's expense' (ibid., p. 144). At the same time, this driver, always on the go, feels no connection with other people or with his environment. Earth is too mundane to hold him back. The yuppie appeal of such connotations is obvious. Nevertheless, Gitlin believes that entrepreneurial car-driver commercials help to reconcile managers to their actual dependency on big institutions. The potency of the driver is wholly dependent on his machinery.

The Pontiac slogan, 'We Build Excitement', seems excellently fitted to this set of images. Gitlin memorably describes the car of 1984–85 commercials, shooting along fast lanes on roads with no rush-hour traffic, driven by an unaccompanied young white hero, as 'a sort of syringe on wheels' (ibid., p. 138). He is also intrigued by the suggestion, 'If you are what you drive, imagine yourself as a Renault Encore.' He notes that the Renault driver, wearing mirror sunglasses, does not so much drive as become his car, the sunglasses metamorphosing into headlights. What he becomes, though, is simply another surface, an appearance to be admired by young females: 'Surface is all; what you see is what you get' (ibid., p. 139).

MALE-MAGAZINE ADVERTISEMENTS

If beer and car commercials may be taken to target male audiences in their portrayal of traditional masculinity, the evidence for this assumption has to be largely implicit, a matter of reasonable guesswork. Surer ground is provided by the advertisements appearing in magazines specifically aimed at a male readership.

For a time, when the subject was men's magazines, researchers' energy was taken up largely with analysis of pornographic imagery in those catering for men's erotic entertainment. However, Charlene Canape focuses in 1985 on such 'male lifestyle' magazines as *Gentleman's Quarterly, Esquire* and *M* (Canape, 1985), while Richard Collier, writing for *Achilles Heel* in 1992–93, gives consideration to the first two of these publications, along with *For Him* and others (Collier, 1992–93).

These magazines, christened 'new men's glossies' by Collier, show the influence, to some extent, of feminist ideas and attempt to form their views about work and sexuality in the light of this (limited) awareness. All of them are clearly of major interest to advertisers, who must produce advertising images and copy that take account of a revised version of masculinity. This version must include lifestyle concerns, those to do with, at the very least, aspirations towards lucrative careers and to do with self-image, including a particular stress on male fashion.

Canape believes that there were significant changes to *GQ*'s photo layout in 1983. The previous type of layout was abandoned as too avant-garde and narcissistic. The type of model was also changed. The previously obtaining youthfulness of the models seemed to be taken to offer a less useful image for a readership which was reckoned largely to be in its late 30s. Celebrities continued to appear on the covers, but there were also bankers, lawyers and other professionals in real-life workplace settings, modelling *GQ* fashions. The centring of interest on male fashion carried another perceived problem with it. As *GQ*'s chief editor, Arthur Cooper, puts it, 'When I came here, the biggest problem facing *GQ* was that it was perceived to be a gay fashion magazine. That wasn't the right perception' (Canape, 1985, p. 88). It would probably be fair to conclude from this that a major task of new men's glossies in the 1980s was to suggest in its advertising a world fit for more feminized, 'feminist-aware', fashion-conscious male professionals but to skirt, in so doing, the culturally taboo area of the gay-male lifestyle. It must also be a world that does not exclude female readers/purchasers.

It would be a mistake to believe that the more feminized male, who appealed to and was partially created by the glossies, turns his back on physical and social power, a component so crucial to hegemonic masculinity. Nevertheless, with advances in industrialization and technological progress, the middle-class male depended less on, say, physical power at work to illustrate his masculine power. Car advertisements – whose relationship to a yuppie version of unbridled masculinity has been suggested above – are important in the glossies, taking their place alongside advertisements for clothes, cosmetics and lifestyle products. The subtle but discernible retention of traditions of masculinity is demonstrated even in fashion ads, however. Fred J. Fejes points out, for example, how men tend to be portrayed in a dominant stance, unlikely to be shown smiling or touching one another or even themselves. They may gaze full-face out at the viewer, and possibly at an object, but not at other persons within the advertisement (Fejes, in Craig (ed.), 1992, p. 16). The avoidance of intimacy, a frequently noted accoutrement of traditional masculinity, remains intact – perhaps as part of the glossies' armoury against suspicions of an interest in fashion that amounts to gayness? Perhaps, too, the male glossies' advertising of such products as moisturizers, face cream and fragrances has to overcome decades of their association with exclusively female consumers. It is not hard to see, when this is borne in mind, why striving after more 'securely' masculine imagery must be a key part of the advertiser's task.

GENDERED ADVERTISEMENTS

So far, gender in advertising has been discussed mainly in terms of masculinity, in relation largely to the gender of the characters, of the voiceovers and models featured in advertising and television commercials. What, though, if the products advertised should be thought of as 'gendered'? By way of illustration: in male glossies, for example, part of advertising's task seems to have been to free such products as hairspray or cologne from an earlier exclusive link with the feminine.

Belief in the gendering of products is likely to be indicated by such practices as aiming television commercials for domestic products at daytime audiences. This assumption rests on two further, reasonable assumptions about advertisers' beliefs: that TV advertisers continued to associate daytime viewing with women's viewing in the 1980s, despite considerable upset in that decade to notions of gender in the workforce as well as among the unemployed; that the domestic sphere was believed to be pretty well a women's area.

If products are gendered, in the sense that some are believed to appeal primarily or exclusively to one sex only, then advertising's images of masculinity and femininity may need to be analysed with the further information that these are believed to have particular appeal to the particular sex concerned. We have already seen above how beer and car commercials, taken to be of special appeal to male viewers, offer fantasies of masculinity which emphasize, say, male freedom from family and more overtly emotional ties. The images of women in male-targeted advertisements centre on physical attraction: usually slim, young, blonde models in revealing clothing, their role largely being to admire and respond sexually to masculinity. Women in female-targeted advertisements have usually not achieved the physical attractiveness that is part of the male fantasy of the female. One of the prime concerns of female-advertisement women is first the achievement and then the maintenance of physical desirability. The common ground is that both these types of advertising take patriarchy as the norm.

Some would argue that the gendering of products is less sure from the start of the 1990s. Coors, for example, starts to target women as beer-drinkers. (This can be seen as a reversal of the Miller Brewing Company's highly successful campaign in the 1970s to get men to drink Lite beer.) Procter and Gamble advertisements woo males as well as females. Advertisers now have to find a balance, so that with the widening of targeting they do not alienate the original, and still primary, gender targeted.

To counterbalance this sort of argument, we should note that research was carried out in 1986 by Iyer and Debevec which seemed to show that products were generally perceived as either masculine or feminine, but seldom both or neither (Bellizzi and Milner, 1991, p. 72). Furthermore advertisers, by electing to advertise their products on, for instance, TV programmes that deliver gender-specific audiences, in effect maintain the traditional gendering of their products. Fast-food commercials, as well as those for alcohol and cars, are particularly associated with televised sports programmes, and thus with their believed guaranteed male audiences.

Still, as yet another counterbalance, this time to the implications of the last observation, it has been noted that both men and women react positively and similarly to male-explicit positions in advertising (ibid., p. 78). Moreover, 'male' advertising may be employed to sell products to what advertisers would conceive of as liberated women. Baudrillard goes so far as to separate gendered advertising from social gender: 'The relationship of the Masculine and the Feminine to real men and women is relatively arbitrary' (Baudrillard, in Kervin, 1990, p. 170).

Denise Kervin takes the gendering of advertisements as much more than a concern with characters, products and target audiences. She believes that gender influences the choice and use of such aesthetic codes as lighting and colour, non-verbal codes such as facial expression and body stance, and codes indicative of social roles and their power differentials (Kervin, 1990, p. 54). Thus, for her, gender coding can be operative even when no human beings are present in an advertisement.

This takes us on to the question of gendered 'reading' of advertisements. As with movie-audience identifications, we should beware of assuming that male viewers identify only with male characters in male-targeted and other advertisements. Men can reject the fantasy on offer, just as women can and do in female-targeted advertisements. In other words, advertising does not reflect or, for that matter, dictate the living of real lives. What analysis of it is likely to show is cultural perceptions of masculinity and femininity, ideology rather than social history.

In more recent advertising, what were once the binary opposites of masculinity and femininity have become less so, have occasionally turned into more fluid elements with more permeable boundaries. In 1988, Daniel J. Bretl and Joanne Cantor claim, 'Although many differences remain, advertisements seem to be presenting a less sexist and more equal view of the roles of men and women in society' (1988, p. 607). Yet, they immediately follow this statement up with a caution about simplistic reading in terms of manifest content. Rather than resting happy with an interpretation that, if the world imaged in advertising is more egalitarian in gender terms, so is the real world, we might consider that this apparent equalizing of men and women is more probably an effect of advancing consumerism. If it is the case that consumerism feminizes by making potential consumers of both sexes, then we should recall a significant aspect of that process. Men are increasingly and unapologetically objectified, both in terms of erotic spectacle and as targets of advertising for products beyond cars and beer, including many items once thought to be marketed for women alone. Perhaps it is not that women have gained a measure of equality in access to social and economic power. Perhaps, rather, men have joined women in some measure – in powerlessness.

IN CONCLUSION

At first sight, advertising in general, television commercials in particular, seems easy to characterize as not only featuring blatant gender stereotyping but as inculcating stereotypical attitudes and behaviour along with promotion of their products.

It is undeniably true that, up to the mid-1980s' at the very least, US advertising depended on an image of the male as dominant, socially and economically. The male of much advertising of that time is in fantasy a frontiersman, either from the past or projected into the future, his horse turned into a car, but with his autonomous, emotionally independent characteristics intact. Women are part of that male fantasy only as decorative, approving objects, the primary interest being reserved for a homosocial group of men or, more accurately, for the product promoted in masculine terms.

The picture achieves more light and shade when it is conceded that the most obviously hegemonic images of masculinity are reserved for those products most squarely targeted at men alone, especially in the context of television sports-watching. Male authority has relevance also to the appeal of commercials for female-targeted products. Yet, it is not the only means by which such products are promoted. The reassurance and warmth of a 'maternal' female voice are valued in male-specific as well as female-specific contexts. Authoritativeness is not the only means of persuasion for the consumer.

The paradox of masculine power and independence in the context of consumerism is increasingly exposed until, in the 1990s', men in advertisements may be objects of contemptuous irony and may be as sexually objectified as women in past examples. The difference between male advertising images after and before the mid-1980s is partly as indicated – that the deflation of the male ego is so prevalent and performed with such impunity in the later period. Yet, what 1990s' imagery reveals about the male is no less true of him in the 1970s', for example, just because it is concealed at that time. Consumer capitalism makes objects of all of us by so often successfully turning us into the persuaded and the gullible. Regardless of gender, advertising sells us the message that our happiness in personal terms is in some way dependent on the acquisition of the item advertised. Men may be depicted as persuaders, as autonomous and emotionally secure enough not to have to express feelings. Yet, advertising, the very means by which the men of Marlboro County and the drinkers of beer are assured of their masculinity, objectifies and feminizes. This was the case for decades before the 1990s'. The big difference is that the secret seems to be out in more recent advertising.

Chapter Seven

Masculinity in mediated sport

SPORT, MASCULINITY AND MEDIATION

The aim of this chapter is not to consider a theme that could easily make a book-length study on its own: masculinity in the context of sport. The context, rather, is the *mediation* of sport – how it is represented and discussed via such media as television and newspapers. Comparatively few males play sports at a professional level or participate in amateur athletics at a sufficiently impressive level to be televised. On the other hand, knowledge of sport and avid sports-watching, as relayed to mass audiences on television, are a sort of badge of masculinity. Discussion of sports often forms a principal topic of conversation in such all-male environments as barbers' shops.

The importance given to sport is beyond doubt. National newspapers normally treat the topic in entire, separate sections when, that is, it does not take up several of the back pages. According to Donald Sabo and Sue Curry Jansen, more print is devoted to sports in the US than to any other topic, including national and international news (Sabo and Jansen, in Craig (ed.), 1992, p.170). Moreover, regular television programming may be moved from its customary time slot or cancelled altogether, the transmission of news programmes delayed, to allow for completion of games televised live. It is not just that sport is given top priority on such occasions, but that it is separated from news in general by, for example, being reported and discussed in the back pages of tabloid newspapers. It is indeed, as it is so often termed on television, practically a world unto itself – the 'world of sport'.

Sports pages do not merely report sporting events now past. They prepare the sports fan for events to come in the near future by providing 'insider gossip' about players, managers, coaches, and likely strategies to be followed in forthcoming games. Sports reports in the popular press in many ways, as Lawrence A. Wenner puts it, 'provide a socially sanctioned gossip sheet for men in America, a place where a great deal of conjecture is placed upon "heroes" and events of little worldly import' (1989, p. 15). Wenner goes on to observe that there are remarkable parallels here with the sort of negatively valued gossip central to women's or society pages. Both sorts of gossip socialize, he suggests.

Statistics back the notion that mediated sport is of vital significance to masculinity. The Amateur Athletic Foundation of Los Angeles found, in a study conducted near the end of the millennium, that 98 per cent of American boys between the ages of eight and seventeen consumed some form of sports-related media, 82 per cent at least twice a week. Ninety per cent watched sport on television. One of its findings was that boys were five times more likely than girls to watch sports programmes regularly. The predominance of maleness, not only in sports televised but among commentators and anchors, sent, it was concluded, 'uniquely powerful messages' about masculine behaviour (Children Now, 1999b, p. 2). Again, in 2001, it was reckoned that men's sports received significantly over 80 per cent of media coverage. Men's events featured on about 90 per cent of the covers of *Sports Illustrated* (Coakley, pp. 370, 371).

It is not surprising, therefore, given these percentages, that sometimes sport itself seems to be a male preserve to the extent that nobody bothers to identify national games as, for instance, 'men's football', though games played by women's teams are identified and discussed in gendered terms. The well-attested links between maleness and sport explain why so much of the commercial break time in national sporting events on US television is devoted to advertisements for the military, itself a bastion of masculine values.

Popular media are often associated with the promotion of patriarchy. The charge is most easily made when these media deal with sport. Thus, for instance, 'sports-writers are key links in a communicative chain that promulgates patriarchal values through idealized representations of male prowess, competitive dedication, and ascetic excellence' (Sabo and Runfola (eds), 1980, p. 162). Or again, in the context of Australian sports coverage,

> sport expounds values that are conventionally prescribed in the rhetoric of war, industry, nationalism and ultimately masculinity – values such as competitiveness, discipline, strength, aggression, valour, implacable optimism, mateship, disrespect for constraining authority and an uncompromising determination to win ...
>
> (Beverley Poynton and John Hartley, in Brown (ed.), 1990, p. 147)

(To this list of masculine virtues could be added individualism, most markedly popularized since the 1970s in the exercise of jogging.)

Mediation achieves its greatest power, arguably, when it is invisible, or when what is mediated presents itself as unmediated and thus real. Television sports programmes seem sometimes to deal in documentary-type realism. The very particular slant on sporting events that is given by camera angles, multiple replays, slow motion and, most obviously of all, by commentators choosing certain facets as of special significance is somehow missed. Mediated sports, which are unusually laden in the process of their mediation with values, many of these gender-related, are seen instead as straightforwardly 'there' in actuality. When events brought to us by the media can seem so transparent and real, then the values that come with them appear not to be values at all, but to be part of the natural world. This is exactly how masculinity becomes hegemonic – when ideology appears to be nothing of the sort but sheer, obvious common sense.

WHY SPORTS RESEARCH?

This last sentence above offers one powerful reason why the world of mediated sports has been taken on as a challenging area of research by those interested in the social construction of gender.

There was a time, most notably the 1960s', when analyses of sport were apolitical, particularly in the sense that there was no consideration by them of gender. There was also a time, the 1970s' and early 1980s', when even feminist analyses of sport treated women and sport as the only form of gender issue, leaving men's relationship with sport as the unexamined norm.

The importance of sport for hegemonic masculinity is but one reason to analyse it. We could recall at this point the words quoted from Poynton and Hartley above, linking the values expounded by mediated sport with those of war, industry and nationalism. If masculinity is the common denominator in all three of these areas, then the 'innocent' absorption of masculine values in the time-out area of spectator sports has a peculiar significance, one that makes it a worthwhile research field. Sport – like popular music for other reasons – has clear political relevance, one that professional politicians would have to be unusually short-sighted to miss. Nationalism and sport arguably draw from the same well of masculine values. If so, then sport, in its apparent innocence of all aims but to excite and entertain, makes it far easier for, say, politicians of the Right to appeal to notions of common sense and the natural, when their brand of nationalism might have little relation with either.

For example, the very categorization of the medal winners of the Olympic Games in terms of their nationality has clear relevance. The playing of the gold-winner's national anthem on the soundtrack, the waving of his/her national flag as a near-subliminal image on some of the visual coverage of the medal award, means that national pride is crucially involved in enjoyment of sports achievement. Patriotism and nationalism are close allies. Again, the Superbowl as represented on US television is seen by, for example, Warren Farrell as a repository of masculine imagery in society at large; the event not only stresses what he conceives of as sexism and patriotism, but it constitutes a marketplace for corporate goods with a demonstrably masculine appeal (Sabo and Runfola (eds), 1980, p. 8).

Research, all the same, should be wary of what comes to seem self-evident. If the link between sexism and mass-media sports coverage is too obvious to miss, sports researchers must still be vigilant against the easy assumption that, for instance, sport in itself therefore exists for the promotion of the masculine. Michael A. Messner makes the point that it is simplistic to consider sport merely as a patriarchal institution reinforcing men's power over women. He affirms that the rise of sports in the late nineteenth and early twentieth centuries had as much to do with relationships of class and race as of gender. His conclusion is that a historical analysis of sport demands that it be as a site of contested social relations among men, with particular stress on race and class. There would seem then to be some tension between a historical analysis and a feminist view of sport, in which its relation to men's domination of women is explored. Messner thinks, however, that there is only a superficial contradiction between these approaches, and that this contradiction has significance only if we believe one form of domination to be fundamental. He calls for consideration, instead, of an 'inclusive' understanding of the way that race, class, gender and sexuality intersect (Messner, 1992, p. 17).

A related sort of awareness of the danger of overstating and of too easily conflating different approaches to sport research is felt by John Hargreaves. He recognizes the relevance of insights from Marxism and the Frankfurt School to the study of sport organized for the masses. Analysed accordingly, sport can be identified as expressing and teaching elements within the central ideology of capitalism: aggressive individualism, chauvinism, sexism. It can also be seen to indulge in the myth of equality of opportunity. Sports spectacle – in other words, mediated sport – can be interpreted to encourage aggressive impulses in the spectators, while at the same time sublimating these by allowing their release through the physical activity of others. Thus, it can be argued on Marxist lines, sports-watching helps to reconcile spectators to their state of alienation. Hargreaves accepts the force of such argument, in, for example, the penetration of sport by corporate capital and sport's highly reactionary values. All the same, the history of sport shows what powerful importance it had to some of the most politically conscious and even radical parts of Great Britain, such as Clydeside and South Wales.

The question Hargreaves is forced to ask in his investigation of sport is why it achieved such near-fanatical popularity if it is, like work itself, just another means of alienation (John Hargreaves, in Hargreaves (ed.), 1982, p. 42). His answer is to recognize that sport is not a monolith, and that investigation of it, by implication, ought not to treat it as if it were. There are important differences to be observed between, for example, professional and amateur sport, or national and local sport. And, presumably, between, for example, national and local sports coverage?

A salient example of research into sport and its televisual representation in relation to gender is that conducted by the Amateur Athletic Foundation of Los Angeles at the start of the 1990s. It took as its aim consideration of TV coverage of women's sports. Its evidence base was: six weeks in the summer of 1989 of local sports coverage on a Los Angeles television station; the 'Final Four' of the 1989 NCAA women's and men's basketball tournaments; the women's and men's singles, as well as women's and men's doubles and mixed doubles, of the 1989 US Open tennis tournament. The overall conclusion was that there was under-reporting of women's sports and that the sparse coverage that did exist was inferior to that for men's sports.

Thus, for example, the research indicated that 92 per cent of air time was devoted to men's sports, 5 per cent to women's (with 3 per cent to 'gender neutral topics'). Moreover, in that coverage women were often the targets of newscasters' jokes or treated as sexual objects. In basketball games, slow-motion replays, with their suggestion of almost superhuman grace and power, were usually reserved for men's games. Spectators of men's games were more likely to be informed of relevant statistics. Broadly, men's basketball seemed to be offered as a dramatic spectacle of historical importance, whereas women's had the feel of neighbourhood games.

In the context of sports commentary, it was noted that players were referred to by first name in the case of women but also of non-white male players. Not once was a white male basketball player referred to by his first name. In tennis matches, women were called by their first names 52.7 per cent of the time, men only 7.8 per cent. Another area considered to be of clear relevance to gender representation was that martial metaphors were far more common in discussion of men's than women's tennis. This in turn was taken to suggest that there was common attribution of strength and power to men, though women must surely show strength and power too when engaged in sports. On the other hand, it was noted that there was very little sexualization or devaluation of women in the commentaries on women's tennis (Duncan, Williams, Jensen, 1990, pp. 1–3).

POPULAR BELIEFS ABOUT SPORT

A persistent belief about sport is that it turns boys into men. It is thought to do so not merely by strengthening the bodies of boys. Immersion in sport also appears to be a form of initiation into the ways of men, whether wishful or actual, in the social world. Through participation in sport, boys are thought to learn, for instance, the positive male values of competitiveness, aggression, physical striving, mental toughness. This belief seems to be illustrated by male sports commentators' choice of language: as suggested in the previous section, though both men and women must clearly demonstrate strength and power in most competitive sports, it is much more common in commentaries to refer to the strength shown by male athletes.

Another persistent belief about sport is that it represents a universalizing force. Thus, commentary on the Olympic Games, for example, refers frequently to the way that it is taken to dissolve national boundaries and such formerly competing ideologies as those of communism and capitalism. It is easily possible, though, to argue in a quite different direction and to suggest that the intense nationalism appealed to by the Games could strengthen the sense of superior and inferior nations. Why else would the former East German state have expended so much money and rigorous training on its athletes if not to bolster its own reputation through the successes of its sporting representatives? Sometimes, too, certain nations' athletes stay away from the Games in order to demonstrate official displeasure with the host nation. Further, it was not long after the Berlin Olympics, presided over by Adolf Hitler in 1936, that the world was at war.

There is an implicit belief that sport in a sense erases gender difference. That is, men's events are treated as a gender-free zone. They are represented as *the* events, no reference being made in commentaries to the gender of those taking part. Yet, what is represented as gender-neutral is precisely sport played by a particular gender.

Women's sport, women's events, are almost always referred to as such, in overt gender terms. The rules of sport, the regulations which define whether one team or one competitor is victorious over others, are the creation of men. Not surprisingly, they fit those qualities and physical capacities most positively valued among men. When women play football or cricket, the usual rules remain in force, as if no other conception of either game could be imagined at this stage. Men are the norm: their construction of games and sports is normative. When there is adverse commentary on certain professionals' performances, as for example when Pat Cash compared women's tennis unfavourably with men's, the relevance of gender is suddenly highlighted. Much of the time it is, because unaddressed, conceived to be irrelevant.

SPORT AS A MASCULINE PRESERVE

MARGINALIZATION OF SPORTSWOMEN

The sports programmes watched by boys in the US tend not to involve women at all. Most often, women appear instead in the commercials for these programmes, usually in background roles or conforming to stereotypes. Some commercials encourage the rejection of wives or girlfriends characterized as 'controlling' in preference for beautiful, sexy women. Female absence from boys' sports programmes of choice and their presence as erotic objects in the commercials accompanying these seem to render sport educative in a different sense from the popularized version of this belief.

The values attaching to gender continue into adult life, where sport and sports-watching in particular play a significant role in men's lives and in male self-perception.

Women continue to be marginalized. Their marginalization is achieved partly by their depiction as sex objects, as decorative cheerleaders, for example, testifying to the potency of the sportsman. The Superbowl could be seen a US male ritual. As cheerleaders in skimpy outfits cheer their heroes on, women throughout the nation at home serve their husbands, boyfriends or fathers food while they watch the show on television. Women's lesser status in TV sports coverage is also suggested in terms of their being supportive wives and girlfriends, whom the television camera will pick out at moments which are particularly significant for the sportsmen with whom they are emotionally involved. Furthermore, when they are shown themselves to be participating in sport, they are given markedly less air time and esteem. The 'production values' are less, and commentators are sometimes convicted of trivializing their achievements by unthinkingly referring to them on first-name terms or paying them 'compliments' on their physical attractiveness.

Most of these commentators would feel unfairly picked on if their use of language were criticized. After all, they might respond, they are talking of women the way that wider society does and that strongly masculine areas of society – such as sport – certainly do. Language does not just reflect social reality, though, it helps to construct it.

It might also be suggested that the lack of quality coverage for televised women's sports is simply a consequence of their lesser attraction as events. Could it not be that the clearly lesser value placed on women's sports is also a consequence of the low priority given to them by the media? After all, Michael A. Messner points out, research from the late 1970s throughout the 1980s shows that sport media have not fairly reflected the boom in female participation in sports (1992, p. 164).

Perhaps, all the same, the above description of women's marginalization in sport could be thought somewhat too sweeping. The 1993 follow-up study of gender stereotyping in televised sport by the Amateur Athletic Foundation of Los Angeles noted, for example, that though gender inequality persists, commentators showed greater respect for women athletes' abilities and less ambivalence about their strengths.

There has for long been a tension between beliefs about woman's place in sport. Underlying the liberal notion of equal opportunities for the genders in sport, there is a strong belief in gender inequality as part of the natural order. Sport is socially constructed, and constructed by men with an eye to those elements believed to be peculiarly masculine in bodily and psychical terms. It can readily be accepted that males are likely to excel in certain activities, females in others. That apparent fact has received another interpretation, though, one that devalues female achievement, because women's skills are taken to be inferior, rather than different. It is as if sport is a natural, rather than social, phenomenon. Thus, because women's bodies and physical skills do not 'measure up' to the maleness demanded by sport's rules, they are thought to be of naturally poorer quality.

This is why Messner calls for sport's transformation from a masculine to a human construction (1992, p. 168). That is why it has been possible to claim that 'the institution of sport functions in part to preserve the unequal distribution of wealth, power, opportunity, and authority between men and women found in the major social, political, and economic institutions of American society' (Sabo and Runfola (eds), 1980, p. 7). It functions in this way all the more successfully by appearing to rationalize its unequal distribution with an appeal to nature.

Sport's special relevance to the maintenance of belief in hegemonic masculinity rests on its celebration of what is popularly seen as natural male superiority. It seems to 'prove' the separateness of male from female and to offer a support from nature for male ascendancy over women. This picture is muddied from the 1980s, though. It is harder to believe in the traditional picture of the purely natural male athlete when corporate and media interests exercise such control over him, as a corollary of his much escalated salary, and when black and female athletes begin at last to increase their share of media attention. This change helps to explain the media interest in the traditional sportsman as a figure of nostalgia in such movies as *Field of*

Dreams, where rejection of the feminine and reaffirmation of the father play such important roles.

SPORT AND MASCULINITY

The discussion above repeatedly indicates that masculinity, in other words the gender of sportsmen, is taken for granted in the context of sports. Male athletes are so securely and, as it were, naturally at the centre of sport that their maleness is not even noticed.

What is often considered to be at stake in commentaries on sport is whether an individual male is 'man enough' to take his full part in the event. If sport is a male preserve, it also plays on male insecurities, to suggest that a player may not be young, fit, strong, aggressive enough to keep his proper place in it. What is positively valued in these commentaries is action, competition, hard work, individual heroism, playing on through pain and injury, but also team work with other masculine males.

The stress on masculinity helps to explain not just the misogyny, but the homophobia not hard to detect in sport. Heterosexuality, like masculinity, is taken for granted. There is no absence of intimacy between male players at moments of celebration. Kissing and hugging as well as back-slapping may be part of the ritual of goal celebration in European football. After the match, players may continue their celebrations in shared baths. Yet, physical bonding of an apparently intimate nature is permitted and even encouraged in male sports only because of the invisible but implicit ethos of heterosexuality. It could be worth remembering here that Martina Navratilova remarked about the discovery of Earvin 'Magic' Johnson's HIV-positive status, 'If you're famous and you're a man, and you have AIDS, that's just unlucky. But if you're a woman, and/or you're gay, that's different' (Martina Navratilova, in Mac An Ghaill (ed.), 1996, p. 133). Homosexuality is usually ignored and passed over as even a possibility by media coverage, while heterosexuality is acknowledged among men and women in sports. Lesbians and gay men are invisible in the media's version of the sporting world. If they are impossible to ignore because they have 'come out', they are still usually marginalized.

Something broadly analogous happens with ethnicity. By far the majority of sports commentators are white males. Conceptions of masculinity are structured around the white male image. There is a wealth of non-white athletes of both genders. Yet, there seems to be a problem about the heroization of the black body, arising perhaps from the use of it in such negative contexts as those of violent crime, rape, disease. Racism is overtly manifested in such insulting behaviour from the 'fans' during English football matches as the throwing of banana skins on to the pitch or the use of racist chants. It is much more subtle in the visual imagery and commentaries of televised sports. It does occur though when, for example, African American athletes are credited with 'natural athleticism', or when people of colour play stereotypical or background roles in the commercials accompanying televised sports.

To illustrate the cruciality of a hegemonic version of masculinity for the reader of sports sections of newspapers, there is a notable absence of photographs of men crying, though we know from television coverage that male athletes do publicly weep over failure. Or, alternatively, there is considerable coverage of the emotional breakdown of a sportsman, as was the case with Paul Gascoigne at the football World Cup of 1990, which suggests that there is something almost freakish about such male emotionalism. Margaret Carlisle Duncan notes that there were seven different published photographs of Mary Decker crying after her fall in the 1984 Olympic Games. She also draws attention to the way that male spouses are shown comforting failed female athletes in emotional distress, while there are no photographs of male athletes being consoled similarly by their spouses or parents (Duncan, 1990, p. 38).

Much more central to the masculine mystique than stoicism, however, is aggression and even male violence in sport. A loss of the will to 'fight', or at least to play on when a player is injured, is sometimes commented on negatively in televised sports. There are rewards from coaches, fellow players and the public when a player uses violence, even if he may be penalized by a referee or umpire.

A precise definition of aggression/violence in sport is difficult to reach. It is next to impossible to agree whether particular acts are 'excessive' or part of the demands of the competitiveness essential to most sport. What can be observed, all the same, is that the human body is routinely transformed into a weapon to be turned against other players, and that pain and injury are the probable results. Death itself can occasionally be a consequence. Equivalent aggression outside the world of sport could result in criminal prosecution.

It is important to bear in mind that much athletic aggression is rule-bound. Athletes who feel that they keep within the regulations in their aggression feel affirmed by that aggression. Team sports create a powerful intimacy, coded socially as feminine, among members of the team. An important function of aggression, therefore, is as a means of disavowal of that intimacy and of the unwelcome connotations of femininity and emotionality. It is not just aggression, but intimacy with other males that is bounded by the rules of the game. More widely, the aggression involved in sport helps to reconcile men to the loss of social power and the taboo on violence in at least middle-class society. (The historical relevance of class to English sport, so that it divides into 'gentlemanly' and proletarian versions of it, each with their own traditional virtues, is usefully explored by John Hargreaves's 'Sport, culture and ideology', in Hargreaves (ed.), 1982, pp. 30–61.)

We also need to bear in mind that it is not just that men perpetrate violence, but also that men suffer the effects of violence. Their shared maleness gives a special, acceptable and rule-bound quality to the dealing out of violence, but also to suffering it – so that customary emotions and attitudes to violence do not apply straightforwardly to those 'playing' aggressors or victims, however real and physical the results of that sporting violence. Aggression within the rules raises few moral problems for players and watchers. It is when it exceeds the level legitimized by the rules that charges of thuggishness are made in sports media.

Part of the important sense that sport is 'natural', and that it extends what are to be seen as men's natural abilities and qualities, is the belief that aggression is a defining male characteristic, that it is not socially learned. If this is so, then sport is merely applying a brake to male violence by marking off an arena where it can be practised more safely. The bulk of evidence from social science would, however, support the view that sports violence, at least, is learned behaviour, which legitimizes but also teaches and generates aggression outside the sporting scene.

Messner comments, 'Violent sports as spectacle provide linkages among men in the project of the domination of women, while at the same time helping to construct and clarify differences between various masculinities' (1990, p. 213). It does not escape his notice that there has occurred what he believes to be a disproportionate chan-nelling of males from the ranks of the poor and of ethnic minorities into sports careers and the more dangerous areas of sports. He finds it bitterly ironic that young black males should be attracted to sports as an arena in which they might earn respect, since this arena requires them, for their survival in it, to be intimidating, aggressive and violent. In this way, media images can be mistaken for proof that the stereotype of the naturally more aggressive black male is a fact (ibid., p. 215).

THE EROTICISM OF MALE SPORT: A CASE STUDY

Beverley Poynton and John Hartley, in an article entitled 'Male-Gazing: Australian Rules Football, Gender and Television', (Poynton and Hartley, in Brown (ed.), 1990, pp. 144–157) explore some interesting facets of viewers' experience of Australian Rules as mediated by television. Although some of this exploration is germane only, or above all, to the sport in question, other aspects may be capable of generalization to the world of mediated sport beyond Australia and beyond Australian Rules football.

Television Australian Rules, it is conceded by the writers, does not resemble the real game. The mediated game is to be experienced in conjunction with predictable, con-ventional images, overlaid with commentary, and such sounds as the roar of the crowd and music (described as 'robust') to mark the end of a particular section of the game. The potential eroticism of the visuals is far more obvious, they suggest, with the sound turned down, so that the choreographed spectacle may be enjoyed as 'lyrical, flagrantly masculine, and erotic' (ibid., p. 150).

Poynton and Hartley feel that television coverage of the game could allow it fairly to be called 'a male soap opera'. ('Most television sports can be characterized as soap operas for men', according to Jay Coakley (Coakley, 2001, p. 372).) Blood (a trickle), sweat (lots) and tears (perhaps, in defeat) are there, interrupted by mannish beer commercials. Interestingly, they note, the fact of some women's attendance at and television-viewing of Australian Rules is systematically ignored when the sport is dis-cussed (Poynton and Hartley, in Brown (ed.), 1990, p. 144). When women watch, the viewing experience is much altered from that which is enjoyed by the implicit, and recognized, audience of men. Under the female gaze, the visual element has an additional possibility – that it may be read erotically. The eroticism is impossible to contain within the usual understanding of the sport and within the usual understanding of heterosexuality in a sporting context. They take the sound, and especially commentary accompanying the televised game, as performing the function of regulating the excess of the visuals. Part of that excess is, for them, the erotic potential within visuals (ibid., p. 151).

By talking of potential eroticism, discovered under women's gaze at a spectacle intended, as it were, only for male viewers, Poynton and Hartley seem to contend that homoeroticism is also there, if much sublimated and unacknowledged. The mediated game sets up a relationship between the male body as object of erotic 'visual pleasure' (to use the language of Laura Mulvey, as discussed in Chapter 3) and a masculine subject, the viewer. The homoerotic implications of this same-sex object and subject are hidden, it is argued, by coding the spectacle into ways of looking which allow the homoerotic content precisely by disavowing it (ibid., p. 149). To put it differently, the male subject may look at the male object erotically, but the programme, as it were, denies any responsibility for this eroticism. It is a private matter of the viewer's choice, it seems to say, not encouraged consciously by the manifest content of the programme.

Figure 7.1   Australian Rules football

The way that Australian Rules players are visualized for television viewers of the game is not designed to gratify the voyeurism of women or to excite homoerotic desires. The text refuses to recognize the erotic element in scantily dressed young men in vigorous action. Men retain their customary position of dominance as spectators, and yet 'the relation of looking and being looked at ... is tenuously reversed' (ibid., p. 150). In patriarchal society, the writers claim, male exhibitionism 'bypasses the reluctance of the male gaze' by denying female spectatorship (ibid., p. 151). Here, I would suggest an alternative way of considering the phenomenon. Increasingly, the male gaze is able to be disavowed by concentration on the female spectator's erotic gaze. To put it another way, if there is any eroticism in the spectacle of sportsmen in action, then the only spectator allowed to be aware of that is the female. If female spectatorship is used to explain the erotic element in viewing, then male spectatorship does not have to acknowledge any erotic component in its version of looking.

Poynton and Hartley take Warwick Capper, Sydney Swans' full forward, as an example of the confused unease that accompanies any acknowledgment of eroticization of a sportsman. The club's advertising agency promoted the image of Capper in short tight shorts, featuring his flowing blond hair and his pout, with an obvious accent on his good looks and sex appeal. The result of this is that, according to their thinking, in the context of mediated sport Capper undergoes 'metaphorical emasculation'

Figure 7.2 David Beckham

(ibid., p. 151). Commentators trivialized his masculinity in their references to this sort of promotion, believing presumably that they were speaking in line with the imagined views of the male audience concerning his use in club advertising. The writers' conclusion is that sex and sport do not mix, except in jest (ibid., p. 152) – and jest is one of the most popular ways of disavowal.

As a footnote to this discussion of eroticized sportsmen, it might be interesting to speculate whether David Beckham's promotion, as erotic, partially clothed model, in men's magazines has had any deleterious effect on the respect accorded to him as star footballer and as captain of the England side in the 2002 World Cup. Beckham himself seems reluctant to disavow his 'feminine side' by joking about his modelling or taking up one commentator's laddish amusement that he sometimes cooks for his team-mates. Perhaps Beckham's refusal to join in complicity with the traditional masculine ridiculing of his erotic potential marks a new phase where sex and sport do at last mix. Or is this too optimistic a view, needing to be watered down with deference to the possibly less liberated opinions of English football fans?

IN CONCLUSION

As sport is mediated to a wide public, the evidence for its connection with masculinity and maleness is immense. So self-evidently does sport appear to be male territory that it is only when women play that the gender of players is mentioned. The rules of sport have been created by men to suit what is taken to be male strength and power; when women enter that world, they may play in segregated teams and events, but largely the rules are unaltered. Commentary on and presentation of sport in television and newspapers show that successful sportsmen seem automatically to be respected, while sportswomen have to fight for that respect.

Not only does sport seem to marginalize women in the interests of men, it promotes a particular version of masculinity that is practically identical with the hegemonic. Aggression, physical violence – albeit rule-bound violence – competitiveness, individualism as well as 'mateship', are all positively valued in the sports setting. Sport is seen as performing an educative role, in turning boys into men, replete with a masculinity that suggests misogyny, homophobia and racism as at least potential aspects of it. One of the reasons why feminist scholars turn to sport as an area worthy of analysis is that sports carry with them gender and sex attitudes that have a vital bearing on the social world. The huge importance given to sport and the fanatical devotion to it by some make questioning of these attitudes unusually difficult. If sport is seen, against the evidence, as part of nature, so is the form of masculinity promoted by it.

There is increasing awareness that the mediation of sport involves eroticism. Hero worship itself has its relation to the erotic. Women and gay-identifying male fans will readily admit that certain players are objects of intense erotic interest. Sport's version of masculinity militates against any admission of such eroticization of sporting heroes by 'real' sports fans, who represent a sometimes extreme form of masculine values. Advertisers clearly recognize and exploit the erotic allure of sportsmen. They must surely imagine that they are reaching beyond female and 'out' gay-male categories to 'straight' sports fans. What enables them to do this is the phenomenon of disavowal – whereby a sportsman may be presented erotically, but this can be publicly ignored. The sports fan can see his idol as erotic only through the eyes of people unlike himself, for example, or can treat the eroticism as a joke, so that the implications have no power to unsettle his confident self-image.

Nevertheless, we may be entering a period where sport's masculinity has to be reconceived. The sporting world is now one of huge salaries, a place of vast 'deals' which remind sportsmen and sports fan alike that players are owned, bought and sold, that they are commercial properties to be exploited for their commercial value. It remains to be seen whether the traditional masculinity associated with and promoted by sport must undergo alteration – or whether, alternatively, disavowal may operate, so that the evidence may be bypassed in an insistent emphasis on what it is more comfortable for the general public to believe.

IN CONCLUSION

It seems redundant to try to sum up the findings of the seven chapters that form the bulk of this book. In any case, each has its own concluding section that sums up what has preceded.

Nevertheless, there are one or two facets of the topic of male representation in the popular media which seem to emerge from each separate consideration.

For example, an important distinction needs to be made, on the evidence cited. This is the gulf between, on the one hand, masculinity as it is experienced in society, or the various sorts of masculinity – whether soft and sensitive, nurturing, aggressive, violent, 'new', unreconstructed – discoverable in different media and, on the other, that form of masculinity called 'hegemonic'. The latter represents an ideal which may or may not reflect the masculinities available in a particular society at a particular time. It purports to be traditional and self-evident, as well as ideal, even when it can be embodied only by such figures of fantasy as the characters embodied in 1980s' movies by Schwarzenegger, Stallone, or Van Damme. Everybody may suspect the impracticability of the hegemonic, at the same time as most people at some level believe in it. Social scientists may find a very different model of the lives that men lead and their gender performances, from the beliefs epitomized by the hegemonic. This does not, though, lessen its credibility as a standard of masculinity to which men are supposed to aspire.

It is important, too, to realize that the hegemonic ideal is not above history and social change. It alters much as masculinity in society alters – dramatically in the 1980s, with the sort of reconception of red-blooded masculinity within Reagan's US and Thatcher's Britain. While some aspects remain, the ideal as a whole may be reshaped to meet different social needs in relation to gender.

Most obviously of all, as indicated particularly by the chapters in Part B, to talk of masculinity in the singular is a mistake. A wide variety of masculinities can be found represented in movies, television, advertising and mediated sport.

Some of these versions are not only difficult to distinguish clearly from femininities – they incorporate aspects of the feminine. Societal conviction that exhibitionism, narcissism, masochism are pleasures peculiarly available to women, for instance, seem to be just that – strongly held societal belief rather than fact. The evidence suggests otherwise. Perhaps it is the function of disavowal to help to deny what in many ways is obviously true. It certainly works in the interests of maintaining traditional forms of masculinity, by, for example, suggesting that the erotic male objects of cinema, television, sport and, clearest of all, advertising have nothing to do with the thrill of showing oneself off. Men don't know anything about that, we are asked to believe. Real men don't, at least. Male objects exist only because there is female or gay-male demand for them, or as a joke (laughter dispels the sense that there might be a serious reason for their existence). Men placed in the traditional feminine position – of what Laura Mulvey calls 'to-be-looked-at-ness' – manage to hold on to their unblemished masculinity thanks to disavowal.

One thing that all the academic debates and essays on masculinities seem to ensure is that it is no longer possible today to leave masculinity untouched and taken for granted as a purely natural essence. It can no longer cloak itself in invisibility. Even thinkers of the Robert Bly school, by drawing attention to the need to rediscover the eternal masculine, unwillingly ensure the questioning of it. If it is eternal, why has it (temporarily) disappeared? If men have to go on weekend retreats to rediscover their manhood, how much of an essence can it be?

Masculinity is a greater mystery today than femininity, as little understood by men themselves as by their female partners. How does a gender which purports to be dominant allow itself to be vilified at every turn in current television advertising, without so much as a protest? Why is vulnerability so assiduously denied by masculinity when the statistics of life expectancy alone suggest otherwise?

This book hopes to have taken one step towards the unravelling of that mystery.

BIBLIOGRAPHY

ANGUS, I. and JHALLY, S. (eds) 1989: *Cultural Politics in Contemporary America.* London and New York: Routledge.

ARONOWITZ, S. 1992: *The Politics of Identity: Class, Culture, Social Movements.* New York and London: Routledge.

BARDWICK, J.M. and SCHUMANN, S.L. 1967: Portrait of American Men and Women in TV Commercials. *Psychology* 4(19), 18–23.

BARTHEL, D. 1988: *Putting on Appearances: Gender and Advertising.* Philadelphia, PA: Temple University Press.

BARTHES, R. 1978: *A Lover's Discourse: Fragments.* Translated by R. Howard. New York: Farrar, Strauss and Giroux.

BELLIZZI, J.A. and MILNER, L. 1991: Gender Positioning of a Traditionally Male-Dominant Product. *Journal of Advertising Research* 31(3), 72–79.

BENNETT, A. and WOOLLACOTT, J. 1987: *Bond and Beyond: The Political Career of a Popular Hero.* Basingstoke: Macmillan.

BERGER, M., WALLIS, B. and WATSON, S. (eds) 1995: *Constructing Masculinity.* New York and London: Routledge.

BINGHAM, D. 1990: Men with no names: Clint Eastwood's 'The Stranger' persona, identification, and the impenetrable gaze. *Journal of Film and Video* 42(4), 33–48.

BINGHAM, D. 1994: Warren Beatty and the elusive male body in Hollywood cinema. *Michigan Quarterly Review* 33(1), 149–176.

BISKIND, P. and EHRENREICH, B. 1980: Machismo and Hollywood's working class. *Socialist Review* 10, 109–130.

BLY, R. 1991: *Iron John: A Book about Men.* Shaftesbury: Element.

BOOZER, J., Jr. 1995: Bending Phallic Patriarchy in *The Crying Game. Journal of Popular Film and Television* 22(4), 172–179.

BOSCAGLI, M. 1992–93: A Moving Story: Masculine Tears and the Humanity of Televised Emotions. *Discourse* 15(2), 64–79.

BRETL, D.J. and CANTOR, J. 1988: The Portrayal of Men and Women in US Television Commercials: A Recent Content Analysis and Trends over 15 Years. *Sex Roles* 18(9/10), 595–609.

BRITTAN, A. 1989: *Masculinity and Power.* Oxford and New York: Basil Blackwell.

BROD, H. (ed.) 1987: *The Making of Masculinities: The New Men's Studies.* Boston and London: Allen & Unwin.

BROD, H. and KAUFMAN, M. (eds) 1994: *Theorizing Masculinities.* Thousand Oaks. CA, London, New Delhi: Sage.

BROWN, B. 1995: 'Black Male:' An imaginary dialogue on the consequences of images. http//artscenecal.com/ArticlesFiles/Archive/Articles1995/Articles 0695/Brown.html.

BROWN, J.A. 1993: Bullets, Buddies and Bad Guys: The 'Action-Cop' Genre. *Journal of Popular Film and Television* 21(2), 79–87.

BROWN, M.E. (ed.) 1990: *Television and Women's Culture: The Politics of the Popular.* London, Thousand Oaks, New Delhi: Sage.

BROWNLOW, S. and ZEBROWITZ, L.A. 1990: Facial Appearance, Gender, and Credibility in Television Commercials. *Journal of Nonverbal Behavior* 14(1), 51–60.

BUDRA, P. 1990: Rambo in the Garden: The POW Film as Pastoral. *Literature Film Quarterly* 18(3), 188–192.

BURNETT, R. 1985: The Tightrope of Male Fantasy. *Framework* 26–27, 76–85.

CANAPE, C. 1985: Refashioning the Male Marketplace. *Marketing & Media Decisions* March, 84–90.

CHILDREN NOW, 1999a: Children and the Media: Messages About Masculinity. *BoystoMEN, Entertainment Media* September, 1–7 (Internet pages).

CHILDREN NOW, 1999b: Messages About Masculinity: A national poll of children, focus groups, and content analysis of sports programs and commercials. *BoystoMEN Sports Media* September, 1–8 (Internet pages).

COAKLEY, J. 2001: *Sport in Society: Issues and Controversies,* 7th ed. New York: McGraw-Hill.

COLLIER, R. 1992–93: The New Man: Fact or Fad? *Achilles Heel* 14, 1–10 (Internet pages).

COLLINS, J., RADHER, H. and COLLINS, A.P. (eds) 1993: *Film Theory Goes to the Movies.* New York and London: Routledge.

CONLON, J. 1990: Making Love, Not War: The Soldier Male in *Top Gun* and *Coming Home. Journal of Popular Film and Television* 18(1), 18–27.

CONNELL, R.W. 1987: *Gender and Power: Society, the Person and Sexual Politics.* Cambridge and Oxford: Blackwell.

CONNELL, R.W. 1995: *Masculinities.* Cambridge: Polity Press.

COURTNEY, A.E. and WHIPPLE, T.W. 1983: *Sex Stereotyping in Advertising.* Lexington, MA and Toronto: Lexington Books.

COWAN, G. and O'BRIEN, M. 1990: Gender and Survival vs. Death in Slasher Films: A Content Analysis. *Sex Roles* 23(3/4), 187–196.

COWARD, R. 1999: *Sacred Cows: Is Feminism Relevant to the New Millennium?* London: HarperCollins.

CRAIG, S. (ed.) 1992a: *Men, Masculinity, and the Media.* Newbury Park, London, New Delhi: Sage.

CRAIG, S. 1992b: Men's Men and Women's Women: How TV Commercials Portray Gender to Different Audiences. In Kemper, R.E. (ed.), *Issues and Effects of Mass Communication: Contemporary Voices.* San Diego, CA: Capstone Publishers, 89–99.

CRAIG, S. 1993: Selling Masculinities, Selling Femininities: Multiple Genders And The Economics of Television. *The Mid-Atlantic Almanack* 2, 15–27.

CREED, Barbara 1990: Phallic Panic: Male Hysteria and *Dead Ringers. Screen* 31(2): 125–146.

DAVIS, L.R. 1997: *The Swimsuit Issue and Sport: Hegemonic Masculinity in 'Sports Illustrated'.* Albany, NY: State University of New York Press.

DINES, G. and HUMEZ, J.M. (eds) 1995: *Gender, Race and Class in Media: A Text-Reader.* Thousand Oaks, CA, London, New Delhi: Sage.

DONALDSON, M. 1993: What is hegemonic masculinity? *Theory and Society* 22(5), 643–657.

DOWNS, A.C. 1981: Sex-Role Stereotyping on Prime-Time Television. *Journal of Genetic Psychology* 138, 253–258.

DRUMMOND, M. 1994: Masculinity from a Feminist Perspective: or How Feminism Helped Construct the New Man. *Issues in Educational Research* 4(2), 95–102.

DUNCAN, M.C. 1990: Sports Photographs and Sexual Difference: Images of Women and Men in the 1984 and 1988 Olympic Games. *Sociology of Sport Journal* 7(1), 22–43.

DUNCAN, M.C. and MESSNER, M.A. 1994: *Gender Stereotyping in Televised Sports: A Follow-up to the 1989 Study.* Los Angeles: Amateur Athletic Foundation of Los Angeles.

DUNCAN, M.C., MESSNER, M.A., WILLIAMS, L. and JENSEN, K. 1990: *Gender Stereotyping in Televised Sports.* Los Angeles: Amateur Athletic Foundation of Los Angeles.

DYER, R. 1998: *Stars* (new edition). London: British Film Institute.

EASTHOPE, A. 1992: *What a Man's Gotta Do: The Masculine Myth in Popular Culture*, paperback repr. New York and London: Routledge.

EBERWEIN, R. 1995: Disease, Masculinity, and Sexuality in Recent Films. *Journal of Popular Film and Television* 22(4), 154–161.

FEJES, F. 1989: Images of Men in Media Research. *Critical Studies in Mass Communication* 6, 215–221.

FINN, G. 1989–90: Taking Gender into Account in the 'Theatre of Terror': Violence, Media, and the Maintenance of Male Dominance. *Canadian Journal of Women and the Law* 3(2), 375–394.

FISKE, J. 1987: *Television Culture*. London and New York: Routledge.

FLOSS, M.M. and SHARTIN, A.D. 1992: Notions of Masculinity: Baochi Zhang at Haines Gallery. *Artweek* 23 (May 21), 21.

FRANKS, H. 1984: *Goodbye Tarzan: Men After Feminism*. London and Sydney: George Allen and Unwin.

GALLAGHER, M. 1992: Women and Men in the Media. *Communication Research Trends* 12(1), 1–15.

GANTZ, W. and WENNER, L.A. 1991: Men, Women, and Sports: Audience Experiences and Effects. *Journal of Broadcasting & Electronic Media* 35(2), 233–243.

GERZON, M. 1982: *A Choice of Heroes: The Changing Faces of American Manhood*. Boston: Houghton Mifflin Company.

GILLY, M.C. 1988: Sex Roles in Advertising: A Comparison of Television Advertisements in Australia, Mexico, and the United States. *Journal of Marketing* 52, 75–85.

GILMORE, D. 1990: *Manhood in the Making: Cultural Concepts of Masculinity*. New Haven, CT, and London: Yale University Press.

GITLIN, T. (ed) 1987: *Watching Television: A Pantheon Guide to Popular Culture*. New York: Pantheon.

GLASS, F. 1990: Totally Recalling Arnold: Sex and Violence in the New Bad Future. *Film Quarterly* 44(1), 2–13.

GOFFMAN, E. 1976: *Gender Advertisements*. New York: Harper and Row.

GROENEWALD, D. n.d.: The Man Question: Foucault and the Politics of Male Sexuality. http://www.newcastle.edu.au/department/so/foucault.htm

GROSSBERG, L., NELSON, C. and TREICHLER, P.A. (eds) 1992: *Cultural Studies*. New York and London: Routledge.

GROSSBERG, L. and TREICHLER, P.A. 1987: Intersections of Power: Criticism, Television, Gender. *Communications* 9, 273–287.

GROSZ, E. and PROBYN, E. (eds) 1995: *Sexy Bodies: The Strange Carnalities of Feminism.* London and New York: Routledge.

HAMMOND, J.D. 1991: Gender Inversion Cartoons and Feminism. *Journal of Popular Culture* 24(4), 145–160.

HANKE, R. 1990: Hegemonic Masculinity in *thirtysomething. Critical Studies in Mass Communication* 7, 231–248.

HANKE, R. 1998a: The 'Mock-Macho' Situation Comedy: Hegemonic Masculinity and its Reiteration. *Western Journal of Communication* 62(1), 74–93.

HANKE, R. 1998b: Theorizing Masculinity With/In the Media. *Communication Theory* 8(2), 183–203.

HARGREAVES, J. (ed.) 1982: *Sport, Culture and Ideology.* London: Routledge and Kegan Paul.

HARRIS, P.R. and STOBART, J. 1986: Sex-role Stereotyping in British Television Advertisements at Different Times of the Day: An Extension and Refinement of Manstead & McCulloch. *British Journal of Social Psychology* 25, 155–164.

HEALEY, M. 1994: The Mark of a Man: Masculine Identities and the Art of Macho Drag. *Critical Quarterly* 36(1), 86–93.

HEARN, J. and MORGAN, D. (eds) 1990: *Men, Masculinities and Social Theory.* London: Unwin Hyman.

HESS, B.B. and FERREE, M.M. (eds) 1987: *Analyzing Gender: A Handbook of Social Science Research.* Newbury Park, CA: Sage.

HOLMLUND, C. 2002: *Impossible Bodies: Femininity and Masculinity at the Movies.* London and New York: Routledge.

JEFFORDS, S. 1988: Masculinity as Excess in Vietnam Films: The Father/Son Dynamic of American Culture. *Genre* 21, 487–515.

JEFFORDS, S. 1994: *Hard Bodies: Hollywood Masculinity in the Reagan Era.* New Brunswick, NJ: Rutgers University Press.

KERVIN, D. 1990: Advertising Masculinity: The Representation of Males in *Esquire* Advertisements. *Journal of Communication Inquiry* 14(1), 51–70.

KIBBY, M. 1996: Cyborgasm: Machines and Male Hysteria in the Cinema of the Eighties. *Journal of Interdisciplinary Gender Studies* 1(2), 139–146.

KIBBY, M.: Representing Masculinity, http://www.newcastle.edu.au/department/so/represen.htm, 1–6.

KIBBY, M. 1998: Nostalgia for the Masculine: Onward to the Past in the Sports Films of the Eighties. *Canadian Journal of Film Studies* 7(1), 16–28.

KIBBY, M. and COSTELLO, B. 1999: Displaying the Phallus: Masculinity and the Performance of Sexuality on the Internet. *Men & Masculinities* 1(4), 352–364.

KIMMEL, M.S. (ed.) 1987: *Changing Men: New Directions in Research on Men and Masculinity.* Newbury Park, CA, Beverly Hills, London, New Delhi: Sage.

KUNZ, D. 1990: Oliver Stone's Film Adaptation of *Born on the Fourth of July*: Redefining Masculine Heroism. *War, Literature, and the Arts* 2(2), 1–25.

LANDESMAN, C. 2002: Lad, Dad and Glad … Now Men Can Have it All. *Sunday Times* (March 31), News Review.

LEHMAN, P. (ed.) 2001: *Masculinity, Bodies, Movies, Culture.* New York and London: Routledge.

LEWIS, G. 1983: *Real Men Like Violence: Australian Men, Media and Violence.* Kenthurst: Kangaroo Press.

LOVDAL, L.T. 1989: Sex Role Messages in Television Commercials: An Update. *Sex Roles* 21(11/12), 715–724.

MAC AN GHAILL, M. (ed.) 1996: *Understanding Masculinities: Social Relations and Cultural Arenas.* Buckingham and Philadelphia: Open University Press.

MACCABE, C. (ed.) 1986: *High Culture/Low Culture: Analyzing Popular Television and Film.* Manchester: Manchester University Press.

MACKINNON, K. 1992: *The Politics of Popular Representation: Reagan, Thatcher, AIDS and the Movies.* Madison, NJ: Fairleigh Dickinson University Press.

MACKINNON, K. 1997: *Uneasy Pleasures: The Male as Erotic Object.* London: Cygnus Arts.

MACKINNON, K. 2002: *Love, Tears, and the Male Spectator.* Madison, NJ: Fairleigh Dickinson University Press.

MATTHEWS, N. 2000: *Comic Politics: Gender in Hollywood Comedy After the New Right.* Manchester and New York: Manchester University Press.

MAURER, B. 1992: Striking Out Gender: Getting to First Base with Bill Brown. *Public Culture* 4(2), 143–147.

MCARTHUR, L.Z. and RESKO, B.G. 1975: The Portrayal of Men and Women in American Television Commercials. *Journal of Social Psychology* 97, 209–220.

MCGHEE, P.E. and FRUEH, T. 1980: Television Viewing and the Learning of Sex-Role Stereotypes. *Sex Roles* 6(2), 179–188.

MELLEN, J. 1978: *Big Bad Wolves: Masculinity in the American Film.* London: Elm Tree Books/Hamish Hamilton Ltd.

MESSNER, M.A. 1990: When Bodies are Weapons: Masculinity and Violence in Sport. *International Review for the Sociology of Sport* 25(3), 204–219.

MESSNER, M.A. 1992: *Power at Play: Sports and the Problem of Masculinity*. Boston: Beacon Press.

MESSNER, M.A. and SABO, D.F. (eds) 1990: *Sport, Men, and the Gender Order: Critical Feminist Perspectives*. Champaign, IL: Human Kinetics Publishers.

MULVEY, L. 1989: *Visual and Other Pleasures*. Basingstoke: Macmillan.

MURPHY, K. 1990: Made Men. *Film Comment* 26(5), 25–27.

NIXON, S. 1996: *Hard Looks: Masculinities, Spectatorship and Contemporary Consumption*. New York: St Martin's Press.

PFEIL, F. 1995: *White Guys: Studies in Postmodern Domination and Difference*. London and New York: Verso.

SABO, D.F., Jr. and RUNFOLA, R. (eds) 1980: *Jock: Sports and Male Identity*. Englewood Cliffs, NJ: Prentice-Hall, Inc.

SAVRAN, D. 1996: The Sadomasochist in the Closet: White Masculinity and the Culture of Victimisation. *Differences: A Journal of Feminist Cultural Studies* 8(2), 127–152.

SCHWICHTENBERG, C. 1986: Sensual Surfaces and Stylistic Excess: The Pleasure and Politics of *Miami Vice*. *Journal of Communication Inquiry* 10(3), 45–65.

SEGAL, L. 1994: *Straight Sex: The Politics of Pleasure*. London: Virago.

SHAVIRO, S. 1993: *The Cinematic Body*. Minneapolis and London: University of Minnesota Press.

SILVERMAN, K. 1989: Fassbinder and Lacan: A Reconsideration of Gaze, Look and Image. *Camera Obscura* 19, 55–85.

SMITH, P. (ed.) 1996: *Boys: Masculinities in Contemporary Culture*. Boulder, CO: Westview Press.

THEWELEIT, K 1985: *Male Fantasies:* Vol. 1 *Women, Floods, Bodies, History*. Minneapolis: University of Minnesota Press.

THOMAS, S. (ed.) 1990: *Communication and Culture: Language Performance, Technology, and Media: Selected Proceedings from the Sixth International Conference on Culture and Communication, Temple University, 1986*. Norwood, NJ: Ablex.

TORRES, S. 1989: Melodrama, Masculinity and the Family: *thirtysomething* as Therapy. *Camera Obscura* 19, 86–107.

VANDE BERG, L.R., WENNER, L.A. and GRONBECK, B.E. 1998: *Critical Approaches to Television*. Boston and New York: Houghton Mifflin.

WENNER, L.A. 1989: *Media, Sports, and Society.* Newbury Park, CA, London and New Delhi: Sage.

WHITEHEAD, S.M. 2002: *Men and Masculinities: Key Themes and New Directions.* Cambridge: Polity Press.

WHITEHEAD, S.M. and BARRETT, F.J. (eds) 2001: *The Masculinities Reader.* Cambridge: Polity Press.

INDEX

Note: page numbers in **bold** refer to diagrams